D0414634

NEUROLOGY

Cavendish
Publishing
Limited

London • Sydney

TITLES IN THE SERIES

ACCIDENT AND EMERGENCY

CARDIOLOGY

CLINICAL CARE

DENTISTRY

EAR, NOSE AND THROAT

GENERAL PRACTICE

GENITO-URINARY

GYNAECOLOGY

MEDIATION AND ARBITRATION

NEPHROLOGY

NEUROLOGY

ONCOLOGY

OPHTHALMOLOGY

PSYCHIATRY

RESPIRATORY DISORDERS

UROLOGY

VASCULAR SURGERY

NEUROLOGY

WJ Ken Cumming, BSc, MD,
FRCPI, FRCP, MAE, MEWI

SERIES EDITOR
Dr Walter Scott, LLB (Hons),
MBBS, MRCGP, DObstRCOG

Cavendish
Publishing
Limited

London • Sydney

First published in Great Britain 1998 by Cavendish Publishing Limited, The Glass House, Wharton Street, London WC1X 9PX, United Kingdom.

Telephone: +44 (0) 171 278 8000   Facsimile: +44 (0) 171 278 8080

e-mail: info@cavendishpublishing.com

Visit our Home Page on http://www.cavendishpublishing.com

Cumming, WJ Kenneth

Neurology – (Medico-legal practitioner series)

1. Neurology – Law and legislation – England 2. Neurology – Law and legislation – Wales

I. Title

616.8'0024344

ISBN 1 85941 214 9

Printed and bound in Great Britain

I would like to thank Pam and Janis for their patience and all their hard work in preparing this volume, and I would particularly like to thank my wife, Gill, for her constant encouragement and help in the preparation of this volume.

FOREWORD

Those who have shown an interest in the 'medico-legal practitioner's series' may like to learn something about its origins and the history of its development. With this objective in mind I will devote a few moments to the past and I will then turn to the future which is, after all, even more important for us.

I first conceived the idea of such a theme in the Summer of 1994. By that stage I had been preparing reports for lawyers on cases of alleged medical negligence for about five years. I had also been looking at other doctors' reports for the same length of time and it was becoming increasingly apparent to me that one of the lawyers' most difficult tasks was to understand the medical principles clearly. To be fair to the lawyers, there were some doctors who did not always make matters very clear. This, coupled with the difficulty which many doctors have in understanding the legal concept of negligence and related topics, merely served to compound the problem.

It therefore occurred to me that a possible solution to the difficulty would be to develop some material on medical topics written by doctors who had a particular interest in the medico-legal field. The authors would require at least four attributes. First, they would have to be specialists in their own field. Secondly, they would need the ability to explain their subject to non-medical readers in clear language that was easy to follow. Put another way, there was no case for writing a medical textbook for their students or colleagues. Thirdly, they would require a fair amount of experience in medico-legal reporting, analysis of cases and dealing with lawyers who were defending or advancing cases. This would give them an understanding of how the lawyer's mind works and an appreciation of the medical areas which can cause difficulty in practice and where accidents can happen. There would be a contrast with medical books where the emphasis is on the diseases which most commonly present to the doctor. Fourthly, the authors would need the ability to work in harmony with a series editor who was anxious to achieve some degree of uniformity across the whole range of the material.

Having identified these four points as being desirable characteristics of the potential authors the next step was to find a publisher who would be sufficiently interested to give the project the support it needed. This was to be no small task and was likely to involve a very long-term commitment because, after the initial launch, it was inevitable that much more work would be required by way of future editions and additional titles. I was most fortunate to be dealing with Cavendish Publishing in connection with my own book, *The General Practitioner and the Law of Negligence*, and I am pleased to say that they seized this new idea with the utmost enthusiasm. At last I thought that the 'medico-legal practitioner series' would become a reality.

It then only remained to find the authors, commission the work and wait for the results. It was at this point, however, that I began to realise that I was still only at the very beginning of my task. Eventually, however, after numerous discussions with various people a team materialised. When the early chapters of the first books began to arrive it was starting to look as though we really were going to have something which was quite unique. When the final manuscripts arrived my confidence increased still further. More than two years after my initial plans the first set of books has become available and the dream has turned into reality.

This, then, is how the project came into being but it must be emphasised that, in a manner of speaking, we have really only just got ourselves started. For the series to thrive it must be flexible and respond to the needs of its users. It must adapt to medical developments and legal changes. Clinical subjects are a primary consideration but it is my firm intention to expand the series to involve other areas of interest. Indeed the first non-clinical title should appear almost as soon as the initial set becomes available. On a more long term basis, I would like the series to cover every field of expertise that is of concern to the medico-legal practitioner.

Uniformity of approach and clarity of presentation must be hallmarks of the individual titles but the series as a whole must be independent and objective. If we can aspire to these criteria we should achieve a fair measure of success in assisting our readers to give good advice to their clients.

It remains for me to express my gratitude to all the authors and to the publishers for their cooperation. In another kind of way I will be equally grateful to all our readers for placing their reliance on us and for sharing our optimism.

Walter Scott
Series Editor
Slough

TABLE OF CONTENTS

CHAPTER 1

SYMPTOMS AND SIGNS

INTRODUCTION

The aim of a neurological history and examination is to locate the area of damage within the nervous system and then, on the basis of the tempo of the history, to make an attempt at diagnosis. The vast majority of patients with disorders of the nervous system require investigation by the increasingly sophisticated techniques described in Chapter 2.

The nervous system comprises the cerebral cortex, brain stem, cerebellum, spinal cord, roots and peripheral nerves (Figure 1.1). The term 'neuraxis' is often used to encompass the cerebral cortex, brain stem, cerebellum and spinal cord, alternatively known as the central nervous system (CNS) in contradistinction to the spinal nerve roots and the nerves which they eventually form, the neuromuscular junction and muscle, which collectively is known as the peripheral nervous system (PNS).

Figure 1.1   **Cerebral cortex, brain stem and spinal cord with associated horizontal pathways (cranial nerve/spinal nerve roots)**

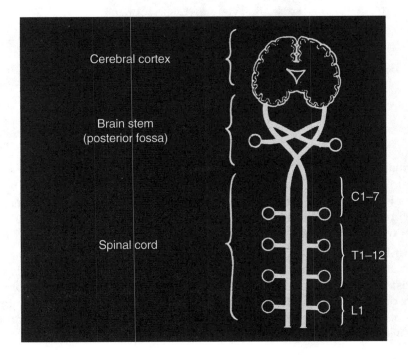

At the cellular level, the nervous system is made up of nerve cell bodies, the axons arising from those cell bodies and the insulation around the individual axons 'myelin'. The grey matter of the central nervous system is made up of nerve cell bodies, whereas the white matter tracts are made up of the axons with their associated myelin sheaths (Figure 1.2).

Figure 1.2   Nerve cell body with associated axon and myelin sheath

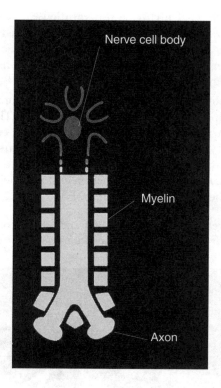

Information is received into the brain via the senses (vision, hearing, smell, touch). The response from the nervous system to stimuli perceived by the senses is either in the form of speech or movement. On this basis, there are therefore major ascending pathways within the spinal cord, brain stem and cortex which convey information from the periphery to the brain.

Similarly, there are major pathways within the brain conveying information from vision to the appropriate part of the brain which deals with the vision in the occipital cortex. The major motor pathway runs from the cortex down through the brain stem and spinal cord, and ends on the anterior horn cells on the peripheral nerves. Activation of this pathway produces movement.

The brain can therefore be considered as a 'wiring diagram' with descending pathways, ascending pathways and horizontal pathways which, within the brain, are the cranial nerves and, in the spinal cord, are the nerve roots. Attempting to make a diagnosis, therefore, is often a matter of identifying the point of intersection between ascending and descending pathways and horizontal pathways.

Horizontal pathways

The horizontal pathways within the brain are known as the cranial nerves and consist of twelve pairs of nerves (Table 1.1). The first deals with olfaction (smell). The second deals with vision. The third, fourth and sixth are concerned with movement of the eyes. The fifth conveys sensation from the facial area and the lining of the brain, the meninges, back to the sensory pathways. The seventh is concerned with facial movement. The eighth is concerned with hearing. The ninth is concerned with palatal movement and sensation on the posterior part of the tongue. The tenth controls autonomic function throughout the body. The eleventh supplies two muscles in the neck and the twelfth supplies the tongue. These are arranged linearly throughout the brain in a vertical manner.

Table 1.1   Cranial nerves

Cranial Nerve	Name	Function
I	Olfactory	Sense of smell
II	Optic	Vision
III	Oculomotor	Eye movement
IV	Trochlear	Eye movement
V	Trigeminal	Facial sensation
VI	Abducens	Eye movement
VII	Facial	Facial movement
VIII	Vestibulocochlear	Hearing
IX	Glossopharyneal	Swallowing
X	Vagus	Larynx and viscera
XI	Accessory	Supplies trapezius muscle
XII	Hypoglossal	Supplies tongue

The horizontal pathways arising from the spinal cord are the individual nerve roots arising from each of the cervical segments in the upper limbs. Having exited from the nerve roots between C2 and C7 these individual spinal nerves enter a plexus (brachial) (Figure 1.3) which can be thought of, to a large extent, as a switching station, out of which emerge the main nerves to the arm (median, ulnar, radial).

Figure 1.3   Brachial plexus

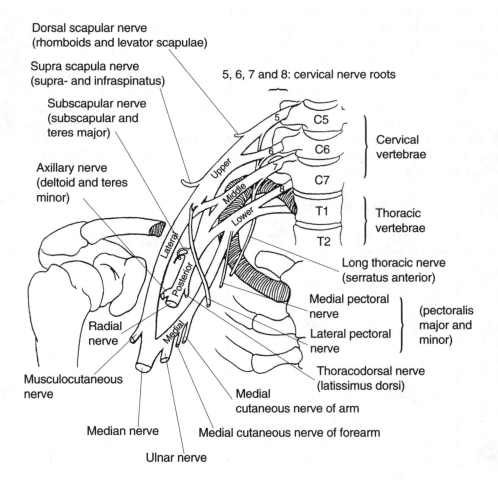

Similarly, in the lumbosacral region, the nerve roots form the lumbosacral plexus (Figure 1.4) before emerging into the leg as the femoral and sciatic nerves and into the pelvis as the pudendal nerves.

Figure 1.4   Lumbosacral plexus

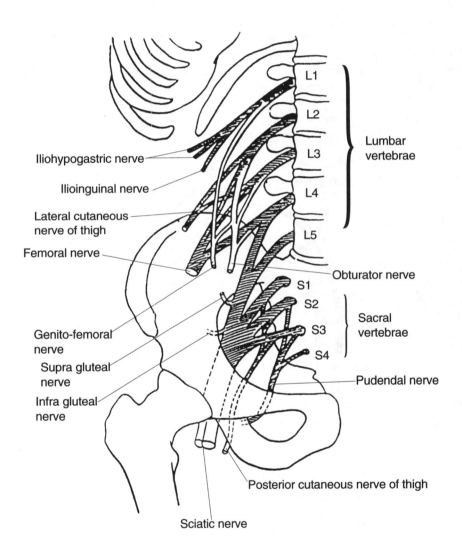

Descending pathways

The major descending pathway is the pyramidal tract (Figure 1.5), the cells arising in the motor strip of the cortex and the axons terminating at the level of the motor nuclei of the cranial and spinal nerves. The collective name for the major descending pathway is the pyramidal pathway.

The pyramidal pathway arising from the right side of the brain supplies the left side of the body and the change of direction of the pyramidal pathway occurs in the lower part of the medulla in the so called 'pyramidal decussation'. In the ascending pathways, posterior column modalities do not cross, whereas spinothalamic modalities cross within the spinal cord, usually within two or three segments above or below the equivalent root; thus, for example, information coming in via the right D12 will cross over to the left spinothalamic tract somewhere between D10 and D8.

Figure 1.5   Pyramidal tract

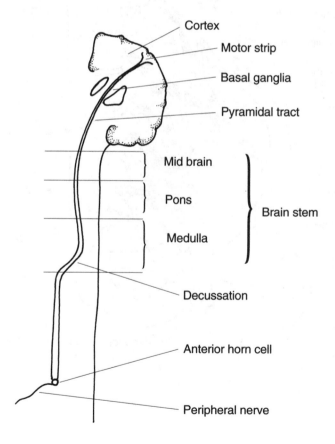

Ascending pathways

Sensation from the periphery is conveyed via the spinal cord to the brain in two major sensory pathways, the spinothalamic pathway and the posterior columns (Figure 1.6a and b). The latter are mainly concerned with that type of sensation which makes the body aware of where it is in space (joint position sense), whereas the spinothalamic pathways are predominantly concerned with mediation of touch, temperature and pain. The posterior columns terminate in the cerebellum whereas the spinothalamic fibres relay in the thalamus and then relay further to the cortex.

Figure 1.6a   Spinothalamic pathway

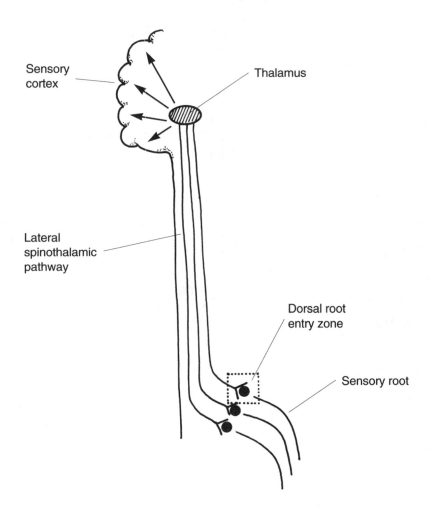

Figure 1.6b   Posterior columns

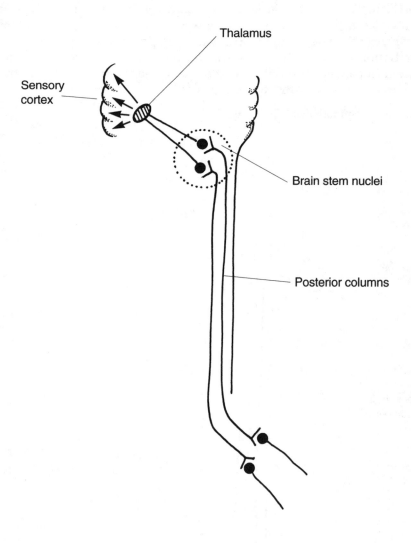

FUNCTION AND DYSFUNCTION

The cerebral cortices are specialised in their functions, as shown in Figure 1.7. The posterior parts of both hemispheres relate to vision. In the left hemisphere, the middle third of the hemisphere is concerned predominantly with the understanding and production of speech. In the right hemisphere, the middle third is concerned predominantly with the body's relationship with extra-personal space.

The temporal lobes on either side are concerned with memory and the frontal lobes are concerned with emotion and the planning and execution of voluntary tasks.

Figure 1.7   Cerebral cortices

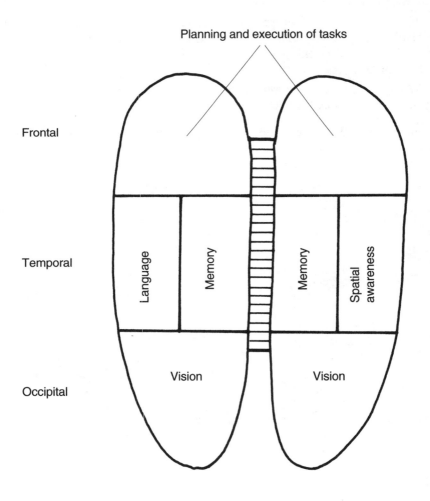

DISORDERS OF HIGHER INTELLECTUAL FUNCTION

Language comprehension and production is a function of the left hemisphere. Even in left handed individuals (sinstrals), 95% of such individuals still have language contained within the left hemisphere.

When an object is perceived by the retina, the information is relayed by the optic nerves to the occipital lobes (Figure 1.8: I), where primary visual processes occur (that is, horizontal/vertical tilting). The information is then passed into the visual association area, where it is matched with previously stored visual information. The information is then transported to the angular gyrus (Figure 1.8: II).

The word associated with the visual imagery is recalled from the memory stores in the temporal lobe (Figure 1.8: III) and the functional connotation from the parietal lobe (Figure 1.8: IV).

The information from body language is perceived from the right hemisphere and transferred via the corpus callosum, the major white matter tract which connects the two hemispheres, and all this information is collated in the angular gyrus.

When the appropriate information has been assembled, it is transferred via the arcuate fasciculus to the motor strip (Figure 1.8: V).

Figure 1.8   Visual recognition and language production

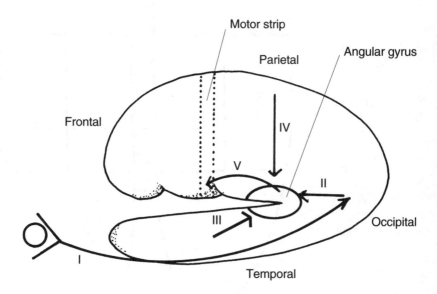

It is clear that there are many sites where interruption of this information flow can take place, which leads to specific language abnormalities. If there is damage to the angular gyrus, then, although speech can be heard, it is not connected with other modalities and therefore no information, or degraded information, is passed to the motor strip. In this situation, if a patient is, for example, asked to name a pencil, they may look totally blank, totally unable to find an appropriate word. However, sometimes they will get into the right category and will, for example, say something like a 'tree' (on the principle that it is thin and upright) these being known as paraphrasic substitutions. The brain appears to abhor a vacuum and, hence, many patients will attempt to 'cover' their inability to comprehend by long rambling sentences which 'skate round' the word – circumlocution. Thus, for example, a patient may not be able to name a pencil but will go into great detail about its function.

The severity of the disorder depends upon the severity of the insult to the brain.

Contained in the same area are those parts of the brain which specialise in the ability to calculate, to read, to write and to distinguish right from left. Hence, in addition to the word-finding difficulty, there may well be difficulty with writing (dysgraphism), with reading (dyslexia), with calculation (dyscalculia) and with right/left orientation.

Given that the angular gyrus lies behind the motor and the sensory strip, the disorder of higher intellectual function is not associated with any disturbance of the main ascending or descending pathways and hence, unless specifically looked for, disorders in this area can easily be 'missed'.

When a lesion involves the more anterior part of the brain and involves language production (Figure 1.9), then the situation pertains where the patient can fully understand all that is said and can make an attempt to respond but, because of involvement of the motor pathway, is unable to produce any words. Because the descending motor pathway (the pyramidal tract) is involved there will then be a weakness on the opposite (contralateral) side with the patient having, in addition to their speech production abnormalities, varying degrees of weakness down the right side (hemiparesis), varying from mild to complete (stroke).

The middle third of the right hemisphere is specialised for body awareness. If there is an abnormality in the posterior part, not involving the major ascending and descending pathways, then patients will often lose the ability to find their way from point to point. In its severest form, in their own house, they will leave the living room to go the kitchen and end up in the bathroom. In its mildest form, when out of their home they will not be able to recognise their way between two well known places, for example, home and shops and will become 'lost'.

Figure 1.9   Lesion involving anterior part of the brain

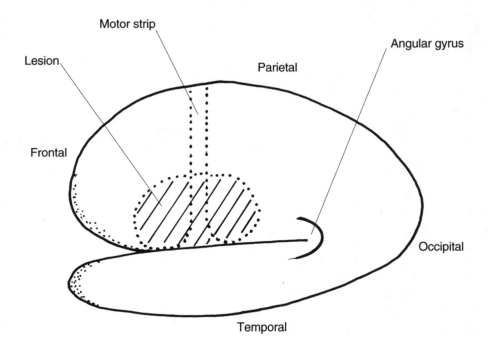

Similarly, they can develop an apraxia (loss of the ability to carry out a specific task in the presence of retained physical ability so to do). This is most commonly seen in dressing apraxia, where patients cannot dress themselves and will attempt, for example, to put on their trousers over their head or their coat onto their legs.

More anterior lesions of the right hemisphere middle third will be associated with abnormalities of sensation, from involvement of the ascending sensory pathway, and weakness, from involvement of the descending motor pathway. Such patients often deny that they have a left side to their body thus, for example, when eating they would only eat the food on the right side of the plate, their left upper limb will fall uselessly at their side and if asked to move it they cannot do so, denying that one exists. Because of involvement of the sensory pathways, when information is presented to both eyes simultaneously they are unaware of the left sided stimulus (visual extinction), but when the vision in each eye is tested independently they are aware of the left side. Similarly, when touch is applied to both sides of the body simultaneously, they are unaware of the left side (tactile extinction) whereas, when each side of the body is tested independently, they are aware of sensation on both sides.

Abnormalities of right hemisphere function are, in many ways, more devastating than left sided dysfunction and patients with severe right hemisphere involvement are rarely able to lead an independent existence. Damage to the frontal lobes leads to emotional lability and loss of the ability to sequence movement. In addition, there are centres within the frontal lobe which govern the highest functioning of the bladder and damage in this area can lead to inappropriate voiding.

Loss of the ability to plan associated with frontal lobe damage, when it occurs in isolation from other damage to the higher functions, can be of major significance for the patient in that, despite retained intellect, they are unable to function effectively. These disorders of higher intellectual function are assessed using neuropsychometric techniques (see Chapter 2).

THE ASCENDING AND DESCENDING PATHWAYS

It is axiomatic in neurology that there is loss of function at the level of the lesion with disturbed function beneath the level of the lesion. Hence, if the pyramidal pathway, the major descending motor pathway, is disturbed at any level from cortex to spinal cord, it will lead to abnormalities of power and tone in the limbs.

Tone is the reciprocal balance between flexor and extensor muscles around any joint. Tone is disturbed before weakness develops. If the pyramidal pathway is involved between the cortex and the lower part of the medulla prior to the decussation (see Figure 1.5), then the weakness will be controlateral, while, from the decussation down to through the spinal cord, the disturbance of tone and the weakness will be ipsilateral (that is, on the same side).

Weakness (paresis) of a muscle implies that its ability to produce muscle power on voluntary contraction is reduced. Paralysis implies that all muscle function is lost. When weakness occurs in one limb, it is referred to as monoparesis, and total paralysis of a limb is known as monoplegia. Hemiplegia applies to paralysis affecting one side of the body; paraplegia indicates weakness in both legs. When all four limbs are involved, the weakness is described as either quadraparesis or quadraplegia (or tetraparesis and tetraplegia), depending upon the severity.

In the special case of children with cerebral palsy, where there is weakness of all four limbs but most markedly so in the lower limbs, this is known as diplegia.

The second and equally important function of the descending motor pathway (the pyramidal tract) is the generation of tone. This is the degree of resistance which is encountered when the muscles are passively stretched. An increase in tone is known as spasticity (or sometimes rigidity or hypertonia) and, when it is reduced, it is known as flaccidity (or sometimes hypotonia).

The relative importance of weakness and spasticity depends to a large extent on the tempo of the illness. In a sudden devastating vascular event (for example, stroke) there will be profound weakness initially, which leads to flaccidity, but, during recovery, spasticity increases. However, with a slowly evolving lesion the first abnormality is usually a disturbance of tone, through its various gradations, eventually leading to muscle weakness.

The earliest indication of an increase in tone is often described by the patient as a heaviness in the muscle when walking any distance. Subsequently, they notice that if they sit for a long time and then start to move they take some time to 'walk off' their stiffness. As tone increases further, they are aware that the lower limbs, particularly, have a tendency to jerk involuntarily, often during a period of rest following exercise, and classically in bed at night. When a patient has that degree of increased tone, 'clonus' (when the foot is sharply flexed, rhythmical jerking movements of the foot occur) may be elicited.

When there is a major lesion in the mid brain, all four limbs develop marked spasticity in extension. The back becomes arched and the neck extends which may be sufficiently serious that, when lying on their back, the patient is supported by the back of the head and by their heels (opisthotonos). Such lesions are usually associated with profound coma.

Flaccidity or hypotonia is due to reduced tone and the limbs are limp and 'flail like'. This is usually seen in the acute phase following lesions of the cerebral cortex, brain stem or spinal cord. Minor degrees of hypotonia may be very difficult to elicit.

The weakness associated with pyramidal tract involvement varies depending upon the area in which the pyramidal tract is involved. In cortical lesions, where the pathway is diffuse, then weakness may affect only one upper limb or the face and one upper limb. In the internal capsule, however, the fibres are tightly packed and thus even a small lesion in that area can produce a complete hemiplegia.

Within the brain stem, involvement of the pyramidal tract is usually seen in association with involvement of the intracranial horizontal pathways (the cranial nerves) and involvement of the ascending sensory pathways. This reflects the 'tight packing' of these pathways within the brain stem and, thus, small lesions in this area can have devastating effects.

Within the spinal cord, the descending pathways can be involved on one or both sides, leading to hemiparesis/hemiplegia or paraparesis/paraplegia.

These terms to describe increased tone and weakness do not confer any diagnostic information regarding the patient; they simply describe the situation found on clinical examination (see below, p 28); the tempo of the history, and ancillary investigations, are required to identify the cause of the symptom complex.

The ascending sensory pathways convey information from the periphery to the brain. The special senses of smell, sight and hearing relate to the horizontal intracranial pathways (the cranial nerves will be discussed in that section). The major ascending sensory pathways take information from the outside and convey that information via a series of relays to the brain.

Temperature, touch, pain, etc, are appreciated via the skin and the information is relayed along the peripheral sensory nerves, arriving at the spinal cord via the dorsal root ganglion and the dorsal root entry zone (Figure 1.10). At that site those fibres which convey information regarding the position of the limbs in space (joint position sense) run into the posterior columns and ascend to the cerebellum running ipsilaterally. The fibres which convey information regarding pain, temperature and touch ascend within the spinal column for a few segments and then cross over to the controlateral side and run up through the spinothalamic pathway through the brain stem into the thalamus and hence to the sensory cortex.

Figure 1.10

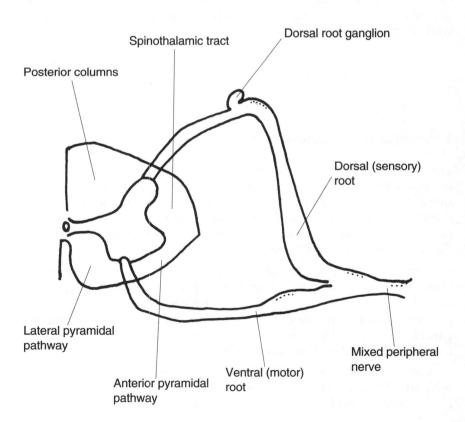

In general terms, damage to a sensory nerve will produce discrete loss of sensation, for example, damage to the median nerve at the wrist leads to loss of sensation in the thumb, index and middle finger, whereas damage to the dorsal root entry zone will lead to diffuse impairment of sensation throughout a limb. Within the spinothalamic pathway the involvement is still more diffuse involving the trunk and lower limb, or upper limb, trunk and lower limb. At the level of the thalamus, the sensory impairment is usually one half of the body. Cortical sensory loss has been discussed above.

When the peripheral sensory nerve is disturbed, initially the patient will describe tingling or pins and needles (paraesthesiae) which then progresses to loss of sensation (numbness).

With involvement of the dorsal root entry zone, the patient describes the whole limb as feeling numb and 'tingly' and is often particularly aware of loss of temperature sensation, so that putting the leg into a bath does not give the same appreciation of temperature as immersing the rest of the body.

Within the spinothalamic pathways, in addition to the symptoms of the dorsal root entry zone, the patient often describes that the pins and needles are 'burning' in character. This reaches its highest level of expression in patients with thalamic involvement, where a sensation of burning pain may well override all other sensory complaints.

THE CRANIAL NERVES

I cranial nerve (olfactory nerve)

The olfactory nerve runs from the cribriform plate, under the inferior surface of the frontal lobes, back to the olfactory cortex. The branches of the nerve run through the cribriform plate to lie within the upper nasal cavity. They are therefore susceptible to damage from lesions in the upper nasal cavity and in particular to trauma to the head, causing shearing of the fine nerve twiglets in the cribriform plate (see Chapter 3).

There is a strong association between smell and taste to produce flavour. Hence if either smell or taste is impaired then the ability to discern flavours will likewise be impaired. In complete lesions of the olfactory nerve only primary sensations of taste can be appreciated (bitter, sweet, sour) and hence a patient who complains of loss of the sense of smell with a preserved sense of taste may well be describing fictitious anosmia.

Complete or partial anosmia can occur as a result of head injury with or without a fracture. Trivial injuries only occasionally produce anosmia, the likelihood rising with the severity of the head injury.

II cranial nerve (optic nerve)

The optic nerves originate from the nerve cells in the retina which run from the back of the globe to form the optic nerve and reach the optic chiasm (Figure 1.11). At that level, both optic nerves unite, the fibres from the temporal half of the retina stay on the same side whereas the fibres from the nasal half of each retina decussate to run back with the temporal fibres from the opposite side. This then forms the optic tract, which is composed of the fibres from the temporal half of the retina on the same side and from the nasal half of the retina on the opposite side. These fibres 'sweep out' from the

Figure 1.11   Optic chiasm, showing division of the visual pathways

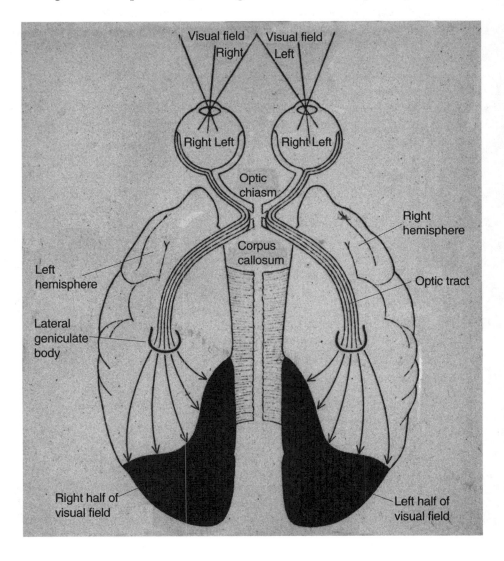

temporal lobe and terminate on the lateral geniculate body, with some fibres going to the superior colliculus. These latter fibres are concerned with reflex activity within the eye, the fibres going to the lateral geniculate body concerned with vision. The final pathway is from the lateral geniculate body to the calcarine cortex in the occipital lobe (geniculocalcarine pathway).

Lesions to the optic nerve may result in partial or total loss of vision (amblyopia). Partial loss of vision is referred to as a scotoma. The exception to this is in papilloedema, due to raised intracranial pressure, where there is enlargement of the blind spot.

In lesions of the chiasm, there is loss of visual acuity, with variable loss of the visual field depending upon the site of the chiasmal lesion.

In retrochiasmal lesions involving the optic tract, hemianopia (literally loss of half the vision) results; if this is complete, it is described as homonymous, but more typically in optic tract lesions only one sector is involved (quadrantic hemianopia). When the pathway from the lateral geniculate body to the calcarine fissure (the optic radiation) is completely destroyed, this leads to a controlateral homonymous hemianopia whereas less extensive damage produces homonymous defects which are congruous. Involvement of the lower part of the radiation in the temporal lobe produces a controlateral homonymous superior quadrantanopia, while lesions in the parietal lobe produced a crossed inferior quadrantic hemianopia. The commonest lesions occurring in the radiation are infarction, haemorrhage or tumour. Lesions in the visual cortex itself always produce a crossed homonymous field defect which is congruous.

The charting of the visual fields is undertaken with perimetry. The pupil is under the control of two muscles which are antagonistic, the circular muscle of the iris and the sphincter pupillae. The latter causes contraction and derives its innervation from the III nerve (see below, p 30). The circular muscle of the iris causes dilatation of the pupil and receives its nerve supply from the cervical autonomic system (see below, p 31).

If there are minor degrees (up to 4 mm) of inequality in pupillary diameter, this is known as anascoria. When there is paralysis of the sphincter pupillae, the pupil is widely dilated due to the unopposed action of the iris dilator muscle. In such a situation, there is no response to light or accommodation (see below, p 29). When there is paralysis of the dilator muscle, the pupil is constricted (myosis) by the unopposed action of the constrictor muscle and does not dilate in the dark.

The light reflex describes the constriction of both pupils when light is shone in one eye; the response in the eye in which the light is being shone being described as the direct response and that in the opposite eye, the consensual response. The accommodation (or convergence) response describes constriction of the pupil when gaze is changed from a distant object to a near object. Lesions of the optic nerve head can produce abnormalities in the pupillary reflexes, particularly the relative afferent pupillary reflex (Marcus Gunn pupil). In this situation, the affected eye shows only a minimal direct response, but a normal consensual response.

Aide pupil

In this situation, there is usually a sudden realisation that one pupil has become larger than the other and this occurs much more commonly in females than in males. The pupil is moderately dilated and therefore larger than its fellow and it shows no response to light, either direct or consensual. However, with prolonged accommodation the pupil is shown to constrict.

The condition is not uncommon, occurring naturally. It has never been related to trauma or drug ingestion, despite persistent legal claims to the contrary.

Eyelid

The eyelid is elevated by two muscles, the levator palpebrae superioris, innervated by the III nerve, and Müllers palpebral muscle, part of the unstriated muscle of the orbit, which is supplied by the cervical sympathetic. Lid closure depends upon the obicularis oculi, part of the facial nerve (see below, p 23).

Retraction of the upper lid most commonly occurs in thyroid disease but can be caused neurologically, although extremely rarely, for example, by lesions in the mid brain (vascular, tumour, MS) where it is usually associated with an eye movement disorder (see below).

Drooping of the upper eyelid is known as ptosis and can be due to an abnormality either of the levator palpebrae superioris or of the orbital smooth muscle. When the former is involved, eye closure is almost complete; with the latter, eye closure is usually mild.

III, IV and VI cranial nerves

At the brain stem level, the III, IV and VI nerves are interrelated via the medial longitudinal bundle (or fasciculus) to allow the eyes to move together as a 'yoked' pair. Hence, horizontal eye movements are described as either outwards (abduction), or inwards (adduction). Vertical movements are described as either upwards (elevation) or downwards (depression). When the two eyes move together, it is known as conjugate ocular movement.

The eyes themselves are moved by the extrinsic ocular muscle, which comprises the recti muscles (superior and inferior, lateral and medial) and the two oblique muscles (superior and inferior). The medial and lateral recti act in the horizontal plane only; the superior rectus and inferior oblique act to move the eye upwards, and the inferior rectus and superior oblique act to depress the eye.

It is evident, therefore, that abnormalities can occur in the yoking mechanism in the brain stem to disrupt ocular movement, or they can occur during the course of the nerve from the brain stem through to the orbit, or in abnormalities in the muscles themselves.

When the eyes cannot work together, the patient is aware of double vision (diplopia). The diplopia is a consequence of the image forming in the correct portion of the retina from the unaffected eye but reaching a different part of the retina in the affected eye. The separation of the images is increased when the affected eye attempts to move in the direction of the paralysed muscles.

The III, IV and VI nerves can be damaged individually or together and either unilaterally or bilaterally.

III cranial nerve (oculomotor nerve)

The common causes of unilateral, isolated third nerve palsies are aneurysms, infarction of the nerve (due to arterial sclerosis, hypertension and, most commonly, diabetes), tumour and trauma.

IV cranial nerve (trochlear nerve)

Isolated lesions are rare. However, a IV nerve palsy is the commonest cause of pure vertical diplopia. The head tends to tilt towards the side of the affected eye. The commonest cause of a IV nerve palsy is head trauma but it may be seen with diabetes or hypertension. Not infrequently, despite detailed investigation, no cause for a IV nerve palsy is identified.

VI nerve palsy

Common causes of a VI nerve palsy include demyelination (as in multiple sclerosis (MS)), infarction, tumour, sub arachnoid haemorrhage, trauma and skull fracture.

It is common to identify combined lesions in the III, IV and VI cranial nerve. If these occur in the brain stem, it is usually due to tumour or infarction. In the sub arachnoid space, it is due to meningitis, trauma or aneurysm. In the cavernous sinus, it is due to aneurysm, tumour or mucoceles. In the orbit, it is due to tumour, trauma, pseudo tumour, cellulitis or dysthyroid eye disease.

V cranial nerve (trigeminal nerve)

Predominantly, the V nerve carries sensation from the face and the meninges back into the brain. It does, however, have a small motor component supplying the temporalis muscles, the masseter and the pterygoids. As its name implies, the trigeminal nerve is divided into three branches, the ophthalmic, maxillary and mandibular (Figure 1.12).

Figure 1.12 Areas of the face from which the trigeminal nerve caries sensation

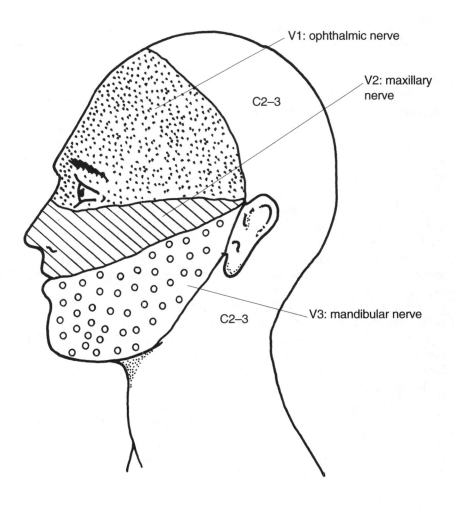

C2–3: second and third cervical nerves

There are numerous causes of lesions of the V nerve and at the brain stem level: tumours, arteriovenous malformations, vascular disease and syringomyelia, affecting anywhere in the pons, medulla or upper cervical cord, will interfere with the trigeminal sensory nucleus and give a sensory neuropathy. Lesions at the lower end of the medulla and upper cervical cord affect the spinal tract of the trigeminal nerve which produces a typical 'onion skin' sensory disturbance that progresses from the nose to the ear.

Trigeminal neuralgia (tic douloureux)

This is defined as a disorder with paroxysmal brief attacks of severe pain, within the distribution of one or more divisions of the trigeminal nerve, but without evidence of organic disease of the nerve. This latter fact is of major importance in medico-legal practice since the diagnosis of trigeminal neuralgia must be made with adherence to the strict criteria outline above.

The pain is short lived and severe. It usually arises initially, and is sometimes confined to, one division of the nerve. The pain is often described as being like a red hot needle and is frequently precipitated by cold wind on the face, touching or washing the face, applying make-up, shaving, talking, swallowing and chewing. Many patients have a definite area on the face which regularly and reliably precipitates the attack of pain. One patient who was seen recently had not shaved over this 'trigger area' and appeared with a large tuft of beard confined to the middle of his face on the affected side. The pain *never* crosses the mid line to affect the other side. In the early stages, long remissions are the rule.

Very rarely, trigeminal neuralgia is associated with an underlying organic lesion, typically MS, a vascular lesion or a neuroma of the nerve. It has been argued that the development of trigeminal neuralgia in the younger patient (where it is uncommon) usually indicates that the disease is due to MS or some other structural pathology, whereas this is much less likely in the 55+ age group, where the disease is commonest. There have, however, been contrary views to this. However, all patients with trigeminal neuralgia merit imaging of the brain (see Chapter 2) to exclude underlying structural pathology.

Various treatment modalities are available. The use of carbamazepine (with the attendant risk of side effects) has been the mainstay of treatment for many years. Radio frequency thermocoagulation of the gasserian ganglion is now widely practised as, with ever increasing popularity, is a posterior fossa exploration, when an artery is often found lying in close proximity to the nerve.

Herpes zoster (shingles) ophthalmicus

This classically affects the ophthalmic division of the V cranial nerve and, particularly in the elderly, is one of the commonest causes of post herpetic neuralgia. The local complications of the acute phase of the disorder are predominantly ophthalmic in nature.

Trigeminal sensory neuropathy

This is a rare condition, in which there is pain and sensory loss either unilaterally or bilaterally on the face, and for which no cause can be found, despite intensive investigation.

VII cranial nerve (facial nerve)

This is a predominantly motor nerve, although there is a small sensory component supplying sensation to the external acoustic meatus. Running in conjunction with the nerve is the chorda tympani, which carries sensation from the anterior two thirds of the tongue.

Facial weakness can be due to supranuclear involvement, where the movements of the lower face are much more affected than the upper face, and there may be complete sparring of the muscles which elevate the eyebrows.

In nuclear or infranuclear lesions, all muscles supplied by the nerve are affected and, therefore, the weakness affects the upper and the lower face, usually co-equally. Lesions within the pons itself, because of the close proximity of other cranial nerves, are usually associated with evidence of further cranial nerve involvement, and are associated with evidence of involvement of the descending motor pathway or ascending sensory pathway. Within the posterior fossa, the nerve lies close to the VIII nerve (see below, p 24) and both may be affected together, classically by an acoustic neuroma, although other cerebral pontine angle tumours, such as a meningioma, cholesteatoma, chordoma and tumours of the glomus jugulare occur.

Within the temporal bone, the nerve is vulnerable to skull fracture and infections in the middle ear and mastoid. After exiting from the skull, lesions in the parotid gland are common causes of facial palsy. Weakness of the facial muscles is common in myasthenia gravis (see below, p 160).

Bell's palsy

This is defined as a facial paralysis of acute onset for which no cause can be found. It is imperative to recognise that Bell's palsy defines a facial palsy for which no alternate cause has been identified. Bell's palsy *must not* be used as an alternate description of a facial palsy. Thus, every patient who presents with facial weakness requires examination to exclude other potential causes, and only when they have been excluded should a diagnosis of Bell's palsy be made.

In Bell's palsy, the onset is sudden and the patients usually waken to find their face paralysed. The paralysis varies from partial to complete. There is often pain at the onset, in the ear or around the angle of the jaw. The upper and lower facial muscles are usually equally affected. The eyebrow droops and the wrinkles in the brow are smoothed out. Frowning or raising the eyebrow is impossible, as is eye closure. When the patient attempts to close the eye, the globe rolls upwards and slightly inwards, known as Bell's phenomenon. The patient is unable to purse the lips or whistle because of weakness of the cheek muscles. The cheek blows out in expiration and food tends to accumulate between the gum and the cheek.

When the lesion is at, or above, the level of the junction of the chorda tympani, there will be loss of sensation in the anterior two thirds of the tongue. Most patients (about 50%) recover completely, although this often takes many months. If there is associated diabetes, hypertension or if the patient is older than 60 years, then the outlook is less hopeful. During and after recovery, some patients develop so called 'crocodile tears', that is, a unilateral increase in tearing while eating.

It was suggested previously that corticosteroids (prednisolone) improved the prognosis for recovery but controlled trials have not confirmed this. It is now suggested that steroids are only used to control pain and in the first 48–72 hours after the onset of the paresis only.

VIII cranial nerve (vestibulocochlear nerve)

The VIII nerve contains two sets of fibres, those which supply the cochlea (the organ of hearing), and those which supply the semicircular canals (the balancing mechanism). These are known as the cochlear and vestibular nerves respectively. Disorders of hearing fall predominantly within the field of ENT and neurology is only concerned to differentiate between deafness due to middle ear disease and deafness due to involvement of the nerve itself. Two tests are used for this at the bed side, Weber's test and Rinne's test.

Weber's test

A vibrating tuning fork (C=256) is placed on the vertex in the mid line and the patient is asked if the sound is heard in the middle or localised to one ear. The normal individual hears the sound in the mid line. In disease of the middle ear, it is heard best in the affected ear and, in nerve deafness, it is heard best in the normal ear.

Rinne's test

A vibrating tuning fork (C=256) is applied to the mastoid process with the opposite ear occluded. The patient is asked to indicate when he ceases hearing the sound and the tuning fork is then held over the outer ear. In middle ear deafness the sound cannot be heard by air conduction after bone conduction is ceased. In nerve deafness, as in normal individuals, the reverse is the case. If neural deafness is identified, then investigation of the intracranial portion of the nerve by MR or CT scanning is needed.

The vestibular system

The vestibular system comprises of the three semicircular canals, the utricle and the saccule. The semicircular canals are arranged approximately at right angles to each other and their position is such that any movement of the head in space produces a neural discharge which is proportionate to the velocity of movement. Provided both vestibular systems are functioning normally, then the patient does not describe vertigo when the head is moved.

Clinical examination of eye movements

Patients with vertigo due to labyrinthine dysfunction will be observed to have nystagmus on examination of the eye movements (see below).

Vertigo

This is defined as an awareness of disorientation of the body in space. The patient may complain that the external world is rotating and may also describe that the body itself is moving either in rotation or with a sensation of falling, these being most marked with head movement. Patients usually complain of 'dizziness', which is entirely a non-specific complaint and, during history taking, the exact description of what an individual patient means by 'dizziness' has to be explored. Thus, in psychogenic vertigo, patients often have a 'swimming' feeling, a feeling of fainting, but have no complaints of rotational vertigo.

Disorders of the labyrinth commonly present themselves as benign positional vertigo or, when following an infective cause (usually viral), are described as vestibular neuronitis. There is a well defined post traumatic vertigo seen in patients with minor head trauma (see below, p 52) and occasionally following cervical whiplash injuries. In this situation, the patient is aware of true rotational vertigo associated with changing position from lying to sitting, sitting to standing, turning over in bed at night or rapid turning of the head. These patients can be shown on clinical examination to have associated nystagmus in the appropriate position which induces their symptoms, and vestibular function tests (see below, p 33) clearly define the condition.

In the majority of patients, the symptoms slowly defervesce over a period of 12–18 months, but a small percentage (about 20%) develop a persistent dysfunction which can be lifelong.

IX cranial nerve (glossopharyngeal nerve)

It is extremely unusual for the IX nerve to be affected in isolation. Its close proximity to the X, XI and XII cranial nerves as they run through the jugular foramen (see below) means that it is most likely to be affected in lesions where there is evidence of other cranial nerve involvement.

There is a rare condition known as glossopharyngeal neuralgia, where a patient has attacks of pain similar to trigeminal neuralgia but the pain is at the base of the tongue and deep within the ear up to the side of the throat beneath the angle of the jaw. This is often 'triggered' by swallowing or talking, coughing or moving the head. Treatment with carbamazepine is appropriate.

There are only four tastes, sweet, salt, bitter and acid, and all other flavours are predicated by the sense of smell. Loss of taste (ageusia) can be due to a lesion of the chorda tympani (as in Bell's palsy: see above, p23) or a lesion of the geniculate ganglion.

X cranial nerve (vagus nerve)

The vagus nerve carries motor fibres to the muscles of the pharynx and to the vocal chords, and its autonomic component supplies the thoracic and abdominal organs. As with the glossopharyngeal nerve, isolated lesions of the vagus nerve are exceptionally rare in neurological practice, although damage to the recurrent laryngeal branch of the vagus nerve is often seen in ENT practice.

XI cranial nerve (accessory nerve)

This is a purely motor nerve which arises partially within the medulla and partially from the high cervical cord, the two roots joining to form an individual nerve trunk. Where it exits from the jugular foramen, it passes beneath the sternomastoid muscle, which it supplies, and then crosses the posterior triangle and supplies the trapezius muscle.

In unilateral lesions of the accessory nerve, the sternomastoid muscle is reduced in strength and may be wasted. When that part of the nerve to the trapezius muscle is affected, the muscle becomes wasted and the normal curve of the shoulder is affected, the shoulder being lower on the affected side and the scapula rotating downwards and outwards. There is often associated slight scapula winging.

The commonest lesion of the accessory nerve is damage to the nerve in the posterior triangle, usually associated with surgery for removal of lymph nodes in that area.

XII cranial nerve (hypoglossal nerve)

The XII cranial nerve supplies the muscles of the tongue. Weakness of one side of the tongue occurs with damage to the nerve with associated wasting; hence when the tongue is protruded, it deviates towards the paralysed side. Lesions in the XII cranial nerve are rare but have been reported as a rare complication of head trauma.

THE PERIPHERAL NERVOUS SYSTEM

The peripheral nervous system is composed of the spinal cord and the paired, exiting nerve roots (each containing a motor and sensory component) at each of the spinal segments (see Figure 1.1). Lesions within the spinal canal can produce purely radicular symptoms, that is, involvement of the exiting root, either in the cervical, thoracic or lumbar area, or can produce combined lesions affecting the spinal cord and the nerve root (myeloradiculopathy). Involvement of the spinal cord itself, without involvement of the nerve roots, is known as a myelopathy.

In radicular lesions, the symptomatology depends upon the tempo of the illness: the more acute the illness, the more dramatic the symptomatology. In, for example, an acute disc prolapse in the cervical or lumbar area, intense pain is felt along the distribution of the nerve, often associated with pins and needles (paraesthesia) and there may, as a late event, be loss of function. In more gradual compression of the nerve, classically, pins and needles is the first symptom, evolving to numbness, and later evolving into appropriate motor weakness.

If the spinal cord is involved, then the signs and symptoms of affectation of the descending motor pathways and ascending sensory pathways, as described above, would be found either in isolation or in association with an appropriate radicular response.

Given that the spinal cord terminates at the lower border of L1 (see Figure 1.1), then radicular symptomatology in the lumbar spine, beneath the level of L2, is never associated with spinal cord involvement. If there is evidence of myelopathy, then there must be an affectation of the conus, that area where the descending nerve roots and the termination of the spinal cord lie together. This has important implications for investigation (see below, p 70).

THE NEUROLOGICAL EXAMINATION

The fundamental component of any neurological examination is the history, and more errors are made in neurological assessment by paying inadequate attention to the history than any deficit in the ability to examine the nervous system.

As outlined previously, the nervous system has a markedly limited response to disturbance of its component parts and these have typical symptomatology as outlined above.

It is not infrequent, particularly in medico-legal practice, that the patients will appear to be magnifying their symptoms, often delivering their history in a dramatic fashion. In some cases, this is not associated with any underlying neurological disorder. However, many patients, who are aware that they have a significant neurological problem, tend to over dramatise their symptoms in the hope that someone will pay attention to them.

It is also important to recognise that, in neurological practice, disease states are not static and there is often progression, or sometime regression, of symptomatology with time. Therefore, apparent disparity between examination findings, at different times, may well be explained by the natural progression or regression of the disorder; whereas the history will identify sequentially what has happened to the individual with time, with respect to their particular disease process.

Although in personal injury and medical negligence cases, the patient will often start their history from the trauma or event in question, it is of the upmost importance that their history up to that time is assessed, particularly if the trauma involved is thought to have exaggerated a pre-existing clinical condition.

It is the author's practice to take a history from the patient before reading the patient's relevant hospital and General Practice records since, in that way, congruity or disparity between the patient's history and the contemporaneous records, both from the hospital and the General Practitioner, can be identified. It is commonly taught that having obtained an adequate history of a neurological condition, the examiner should not therefore be faced with any 'shocks' when conducting the examination, in that, it should reveal what the examiner expected to find from the area of the nervous system involved. While this is true for experienced examiners of the nervous system, in the broadest sense, it is less likely to be true for non-neurologists and junior staff both in neurology and other specialities, who tend to place more emphasis on examination than on the history.

The formal neurological examination comprises of assessment of higher intellectual function, examination of the cranial nerves and examination of the peripheral nervous system.

Assessment of higher intellectual function

In practice, this means assessment of language comprehension and language production indicating left hemisphere involvement, assessment of the patient's awareness of extra-personal space to assess right hemisphere performance, assessment of both short and long term memory, and assessment of changes in behaviour.

Most of the parameters involved in the assessment of higher intellectual function can be deduced while taking the history and may need only to be confirmed by bed side testing. Hence, for example, a patient who appeared to have an impairment of short term memory can be given a sentence to remember; they are then asked to recall that sentence at one, two, three, four and five minute intervals, which gives a rough guide to short term memory. Again, in a patient who appears to have difficulty finding words, this can be explored, as can agraphia and alexia. Severe disorders of the right hemisphere, which may produce a dressing apraxia (see above, p 10), can be assessed when the patient is getting undressed for the examination.

If, in medico-legal practice, there is suggestive evidence of impairment of higher intellectual function, then the patient should have detailed neuropsychometric tests (see below, p 46), which are far superior to any form of bed side testing.

Examination of the cranial nerves

I cranial nerve

Traditionally, the I cranial nerve is tested by asking the patient to smell various odours (clove, eucalyptus, etc). Ammonia is used traditionally since, even in patients who have complete loss of smell, there will usually be a response to the activation of the sensory fibres of the V nerve.

II cranial nerve

The II cranial nerve is assessed by testing the visual fields to confrontation, by carrying out fundoscopy to assess the retina and the optic nerve head, and by checking the pupillary responses.

III, IV, VI cranial nerves

These are assessed by eye movements, where the patient is asked, having stabilised the head, to track the examiner's finger to the right, to the left, up and down and then, in the far right and far left position, to move the eyes vertically.

V cranial nerve

The V cranial nerve is tested by looking for sensation in all three divisions of the nerve. Testing for psychogenic sensory loss is common in testing the V nerve. A patient who has lost, for example, sensation over the left side of the face, will always be able to appreciate a tuning fork over the forehead on that side since vibration sense is appreciated by the bone of the skull in its totality. In patients with psychogenic sensory loss, there is an apparent change in the appreciation of vibration sense at the mid line.

VII cranial nerve

The VII cranial nerve is tested by asking the patient to elevate their eyebrows, to screw up their eyes and to puff out their cheeks, thus testing all components of the facial nerves. In the majority of cases, facial nerve abnormalities will be noted during the history taking and only need to be confirmed on examination.

VIII cranial nerve

This is tested by Rinne's and Weber's tests as outlined above (see pp 24–25).

IX and X cranial nerves

These are rarely tested in routine bed side testing since they are uncomfortable for the patient and are only investigated if there is evidence of an associated problem in that area.

XI cranial nerve

This is tested by testing the strength of the sternomastoid muscles and of the trapezius muscle.

XII cranial nerve

This is assessed by asking the patient to protrude the tongue, the tongue deviating to the affected side in a XII nerve lesion.

Examination of the peripheral nervous system

The upper and lower limbs are assessed in a formal manner, traditionally upper limbs first and lower limbs second. Within neurology, it is always important to assess the upper limbs even if the patient appears only to be complaining of abnormalities in the lower limbs, since they may be predicated by a lesion in the spinal cord and not be due to a lesion in the lumbar spine. The limbs are assessed for power, tone, co-ordination, sensation and reflexes, comparing the sides.

Power is tested at the shoulder, at the elbow, at the biceps and triceps, at the wrist with the flexors and extensors and at the fingers, again with the flexors and extensors. The intrinsic hand muscles are then tested. Tone in the upper limbs is notoriously difficult to assess even for an experienced examiner, unless it is massively increased, which is usually associated with severe cortical damage.

Co-ordination is tested by asking the patient to tap repetitively on the examiner's hand, the examiner feeling for cadence and rhythm. If this is abnormal then rapid alternating movements will also be abnormal, the latter simply being a more sophisticated way to examine co-ordination. The least discriminatory test for co-ordination is the finger/nose test where the patient is asked to touch the examiner's finger and then touch their own nose. This will only be positive in severe cerebellar damage. Sensation is tested to light touch and pin prick in the appropriate dermatomes. The reflexes are tested at the biceps, supinator and triceps. In patients who have spinal cord damage, there may be evidence of more extensive reflex changes. When they are increased, there may be a detectable pectoral reflex and the finger jerk may be present.

In assessing the upper limb function, the aim is to identify a focal lesion in one or other limb and to look for asymmetry between the limbs.

In the lower limbs, power is tested at hip, knee and ankle. It is much easier to assess tone in the lower limbs when the patient is left lying flat on the bed, in as relaxed a state as possible, and the knee is rapidly elevated. When tone is increased, there is a lag time in the movement of the lower limb.

Co-ordination in the lower limb is assessed by asking the patient to place their heel over their knee and rub their foot up and down their shin. This test is subject to wide individual variations. Sensation is again tested in the appropriate dermatomes. The reflexes in the lower limbs are tested at the knee and ankle jerk, and the plantar response.

In lesions of the descending motor pathway, the plantar response may well be extensor but this depends to a very large extent on the tempo of the history. Acute lesions of the descending motor pathway lead to an early extensor plantar response (positive Babinski response), whereas slowly evolving lesions may be associated with a normal plantar response for long periods of time.

In the assessment of tone in the lower limbs, patients who are anxious may appear to have elevated tone. To differentiate these from patients with organic elevation of tone, the crossed adductor responses need to be tested by tapping over the hamstring tendon on one side which causes inversion of the opposite limb. This is seen only in organic lesions of the spinal cord.

Balance is assessed by asking the patient to stand with their heels and toes together in an upright position with the eyes open and shut. However, the majority of patients with disturbance of the cerebellum, leading to ataxia, will have been identified by their gait during the initial part of the consultation or examination.

Finally, the majority of neurologists will now assess the carotid arteries for the presence of bruits and, if they are present, will listen over the sub clavian arteries and the femoral arteries. The presence of intracranial bruits is assessed by listening over the cranium.

The counsel of perfection would say that the examination is recorded seriatim as described. However, most examiners tend to record only the relevant abnormal features.

CHAPTER 2

NEUROLOGICAL INVESTIGATIONS

INTRODUCTION

Having obtained a detailed history from a patient and having carried out a neurological examination, as detailed in the previous chapter, the examiner should have some concept of which level of the neuraxis is affected (cortex, brain stem, spinal cord, peripheral nerve or muscle) and further investigation will now be required to identify the pathology underlying the patient's symptoms and signs.

The commonly used investigations in neurology can be divided into:

(a) imaging (X-ray, CT, MRI, angiography);

(b) neurophysiology (EEG, EMG, NCV, evoked potentials);

(c) lumbar puncture and myelography;

(d) biopsy (brain, nerve, muscle); and

(e) neuropsychology.

IMAGING

Plain radiology of the skull, spinal, thoracic and lumbar spine remains of importance, even though more sophisticated imaging modalities are now available.

Plain X-rays will delineate fractures much more clearly than CT (computerised tomography) or MR (magnetic resonance) imaging. In the skull, special views may be required, for example, basal view, to identify the foramina at the base of the skull and for the orbits. In the cervical spine, canal diameter, which is of importance with respect to hyper-extension/hyper-flexion injury (whiplash) (see Chapter 3) can be measured only from plain radiology and views of the spine in flexion and extension are also of importance in determining stability.

The ability, however, to image the brain and spinal cord has been greatly enhanced by CT and, more recently, by MR techniques. It is to be expected that MR will become the modality of choice in the future, primarily because it does not expose the patient to any radiation hazard. However, MR is not currently freely available throughout the UK.

CT scanning, and particularly the modern techniques of spiral scanning, can rapidly image the brain and show areas of infarction, bleeding, tumour and atrophy (see Figure 2.1a–d). Particularly with a subdural haematoma, it is possible to identify the age of the subdural by measuring its density (in Hounsfield units).

Figure 2.1a   **CT scan of the brain, showing infarction in the left parieto-occipital region. In addition, there has been recent haemorrhage in the right parietal region**

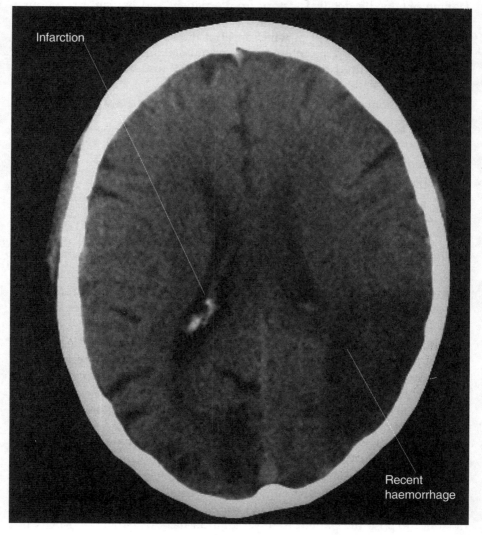

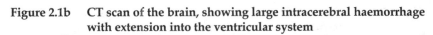

Figure 2.1b   CT scan of the brain, showing large intracerebral haemorrhage with extension into the ventricular system

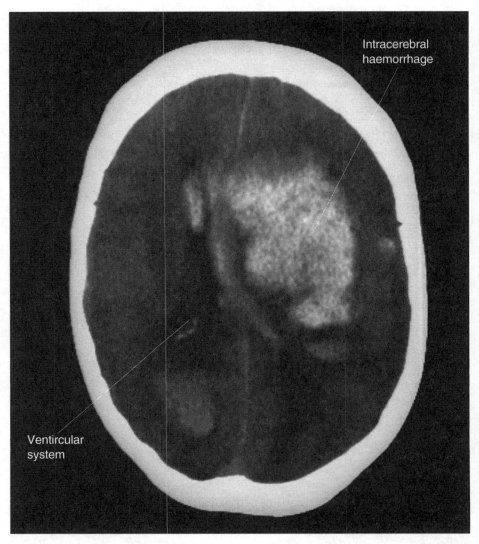

Figure 2.1c CT scan of the brain, showing large hemisphere glioma with considerable surrounding oedema

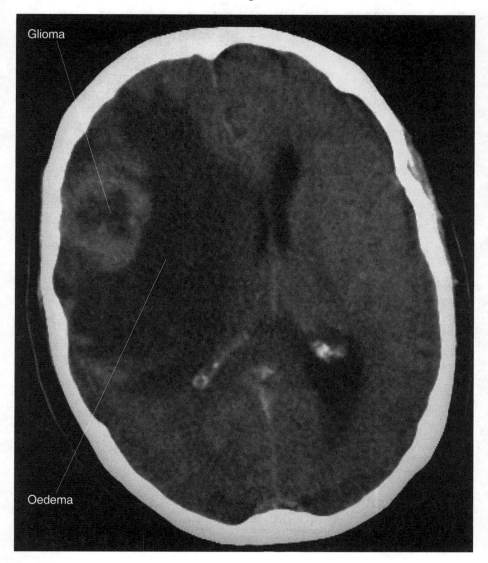

Figure 2.1d   CT scan of the brain, showing cerebral atrophy – note the marked widening of the sulci

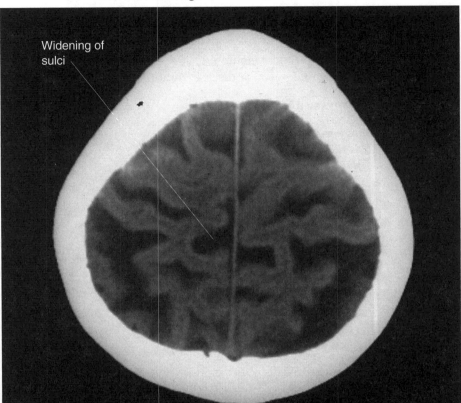

Widening of sulci

CT techniques are not directly able to identify the spinal cord. However, CT scanning is superior to MR scanning in identifying foraminal disorders in the cervical and, to a lesser extent, thoracic spine. In the lumbar spine, CT is of considerable importance in identifying disc prolapses. If the spinal cord needs to be imaged, then some form of contrast media has to be introduced into the spinal cord via a lumbar puncture and then the area of interest can be scanned using CT (CT myelography).

MR scanning is the modality of choice for most neurological diseases, given the greater degree of detail which can be identified without exposing the patient to radiation risk. MR scanning uses a series of different sequences, which are used to highlight different properties of neural tissue. The most common are T1 weighted (see Figure 2.2a) and T2 weighted (see Figure 2.2b). Other special sequences (proton weighted, spin echo and FLARE) are used in particular areas, for example, vascular disease/multiple sclerosis.

Figure 2.2a   T1 weighted MR scan of the brain

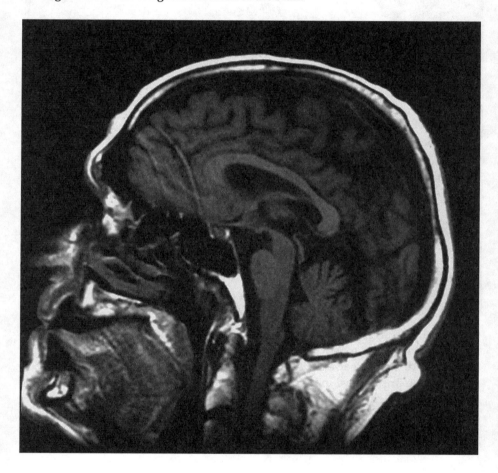

Figure 2.2b   T2 weighted MR scan of the brain

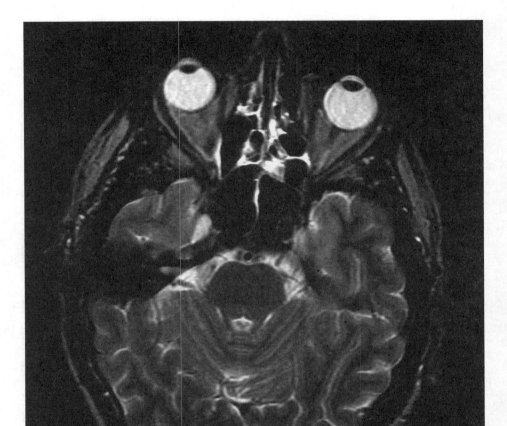

The current limitation of MR scanning is the length of time it takes to obtain a scan and the fact that, for many patients, the technique is very claustrophobic, some 25% of patients require sedation in order to undertake a scan.

However, in the brain, MR scanning readily identifies vascular disease, MS and tumours, and is greatly superior to CT scanning in identifying the structures in the posterior fossa (pons, cerebellum). Spinal MR techniques readily identify disc prolapse and nerve root entrapment.

The most up to date MR scanners are able to undertake MR angiography (Figure 2.3), that is, they can identify the blood vessels in the neck and in the brain. At present, however, the level of sophistication is not such that conventional angiography has been superseded.

Figure 2.3   MR angiogram of the carotid system

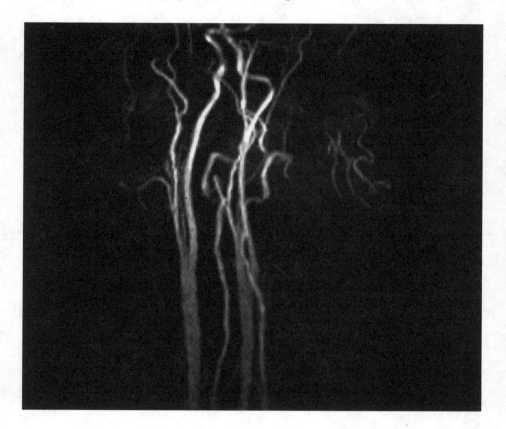

Angiography is undertaken to look at the blood supply to the brain. The commonest technique currently is for a catheter to be passed via the femoral artery to the arch of the aorta; contrast is then injected directly into each carotid and into the basilar system by selective catheterisation; thus the intracranial blood supply can be demonstrated. This technique shows, for example, atheroma of the vessel wall, aneurysms, arteriovenous malformations and arterial spasm. It can show displacement of the vessels due to tumour, and it can identify the pathological circulation within the tumour, as well as infarcts and abscesses.

The technique, however, carries a significant risk of mortality and morbidity. Up to 5% of patients may suffer a transient or permanent neurological deficit following angiography and, occasionally, fatal strokes can occur, particularly in patients with arteriosclerosis. Complications of cardiac catheterisation and angiography are dealt with in Chapter 7.

NEUROPHYSIOLOGY

Neurophysiology comprises EEG, NCV, EMG, and evoked potential studies (VEP, BSAP, SSEP).

EEG (electroencephalogram)

The EEG (electroencephalogram) is probably the most widely used neurological investigation, but not necessarily by neurologists. The EEG gives information as to the underlying brain activity and hence of its disorders. The 'normal' EEG shows a dominant rhythm, known as alpha, which is between 10 and 14 cycles per second (CPS). A faster beta rhythm, at 14 CPS, is seen and does not signify any pathological abnormality. Rhythms less than alpha are usually considered to be abnormal, that is, theta activity at 5–10 CPS and delta activity at less than 5 CPS.

In addition to disruption of the wave forms, there may disruption of the pattern of the wave itself, and this is usually seen in epileptogenic activity. Spike and sharp wave, with following slow wave, may indicate the presence of an epileptogenic focus. Generalised bursts of spike, polyspike and slow wave activity may be seen in the primary generalised epilepsies.

Activation procedures, to try and induce an abnormality in a record, are frequently undertaken. In particular, hyperventilation, where a patient is asked to over-breathe for a period of two to three minutes, is used; this can induce the record to become unstable, and may also accentuate a previously suspect area on the resting record. Frequently employed for activation is photic stimulation at frequencies of between three and 20 cycles per second; this can induce generalised discharges and, very occasionally, may trigger a seizure.

In disorders of consciousness, the pattern of the theta and delta rhythms may be important in that, if they occur on one side of the brain only and a normal pattern is seen on the other side, this indicates single hemisphere damage. However, the use of the EEG in this situation has, to a large extent, been overtaken by scanning techniques.

In patients with encephalopathy (see Chapter 5), the EEG has a distinct pattern of change associated with the underlying encephalopathic process, for example, in hepatic encephalopathy, where serial recordings can be used prognostically.

The most common request for an EEG is to 'exclude a diagnosis of epilepsy'. This can never be achieved by an EEG since, in the normal population, up to 25% of EEGs are abnormal in patient's who have never had a neurological abnormality. In addition, *inter* ictal, that is, between fits, EEGs can be normal, and only be abnormal during a seizure. In the primary generalised epilepsies (see Chapter 6), following a tonic clonic seizure, there may be disruption of the record for considerable periods of time, up to 24 hours after the event, which may be helpful in distinguishing genuine tonic clonic seizures from pseudo seizures. In the partial epilepsies (see Chapter 6), the seizure discharge is confined to the cortex, and the EEG may be completely normal within minutes of a seizure. The only positive way of diagnosing epilepsy on the basis of an EEG is for a seizure to occur during a record, but this is a rare event.

In an attempt to increase the diagnostic ability of an EEG, the concept of 24 hour recordings is now well established. Serial 24 hour recordings can be employed to 'catch' minor episodes which may or may not be epileptogenic in nature. In specialist centres, this is supplemented by video recordings where the patient is observed over a 24 hour period and the EEG is continuously monitored, so that their behaviour during abnormalities on EEG can be identified.

NCV (nerve conduction velocity) studies

Studies of nerve conduction velocities (motor and sensory) (NCV) are complementary to EMG studies (electromyographic) of muscle function.

Peripheral nerves are made up of a motor and a sensory component (see Chapter 12). The speed of conduction and the amplitude of the evoked potential in both motor and sensory nerves can be measured by direct stimulation. This involves placing a stimulating electrode over a motor or sensory nerve and recording from a distant site. This is of particular importance in the entrapment neuropathies (see Chapter 12). The estimation of nerve conduction is of benefit in the investigation of a peripheral neuropathy (see Chapter 12).

Nerve conduction studies may prove unpleasant but, except in unusual instances (see below, p 43), have no inherent risk.

EMG (electromyogram)

This records the electrical activity of the muscle; the information is gained either by recording from the surface of the muscle or from a needle inserted within the muscle. These techniques are of particular value in assessment of patients with neuromuscular disease (see Chapter 12).

When concentric needles are inserted into the muscle there may be a local reaction and pain which is short lived. Occasionally, in patients who have severely affected nerves, when assessing nerve conduction, needle electrodes have to be employed rather than surface electrodes and hence a small risk of local reaction is associated with particularly severe nerve involvement.

A combination of NCV and EMG studies are used to assess the neuromuscular junction, where a rapid train of impulses is sent down the nerve and recorded by a concentric needle electrode in the muscle, the amplitude of the recording being noted. If this falls with repetitive stimulation, this suggests a diagnosis of myasthenia gravis. If the compound action potential rises, this suggests a myasthenic syndrome (see Chapter 11).

Evoked potential studies

These comprise visual evoked responses (VER), brain stem (auditory) evoked responses (BSAP) and somatosensory evoked responses (SSEP). In these techniques, a sensory stimulus is applied to either the eye, the ear or to a limb, and the time taken for the information to reach the appropriate part of the cortex is recorded.

These techniques therefore permit assessment of the II (optic) nerve (visual evoked response), the VIII (vestibulocochlear) nerve (auditory evoked response) and the ascending pathways of the spinal cord (somatosensory evoked responses). These techniques therefore study the functional integrity of the nerve pathways.

Although occasionally unpleasant, these techniques convey no direct risk to the patient.

LUMBAR PUNCTURE

It is often necessary to examine the cerebrospinal fluid (CSF), the fluid which surrounds the brain in the spinal cord. This is most important in infective disease of the nervous system (meningitis) and lumbar puncture is a valuable aid in the diagnosis of subarachnoid haemorrhage. CSF examination can also be helpful in some forms of neuropathies, in multiple sclerosis and in some forms of malignancy. Estimation of the CSF has no role to play in evaluation of spinal or cerebral tumours.

Access to the CSF is via a lumbar puncture. This should not be undertaken in the presence of abnormal neurological signs, since that is suggestive of structural pathology within the brain or the spinal cord. In such instances, an appropriate imaging technique must be undertaken before the CSF can be accessed safely. In most instances, this will necessitate referral to a specialist

Neurosciences Unit. It is apparent, therefore, that lumbar punctures, to examine the CSF, are most often undertaken outside Neurological Units.

There are recognised complications of lumbar punctures, by far the most common being postural headache, which lasts a week or less and occurs in about 40% of patients. Other complications (see below) are rare. However, the prospect of a lumbar puncture seems to cause an inordinate amount of fear and anxiety in patients, which presumably influences the frequency of 'so called' complications from the procedure.

Post lumbar puncture headache, which occurs in up to 40% of patients, begins within 48 hours of the procedure in the majority of patients, and within 72 hours in about 90% of patients, though the onset can be delayed for up to 14 days. The duration of headache is less than five days in 80% of patients. Although the headache can persist for up to 12 months, this is exceedingly rare.

The headache is described as bilateral and can be either frontal, occipital or generalised. It is described as a feeling of pressure which is maximal when in the upright position, and decreased, or resolves, when the patient is lying down. The headache is worse with movement, coughing, straining and sneezing. The longer the patient is upright, the longer it takes for the headache to subside when the patient becomes horizontal. It is probable that a slow leak through the dura (the lining of the spine and brain) is the cause of the headache, where the rate of loss of CSF is initially greater than the rate of production.

Post lumbar puncture headache is twice as common in women as in men. Its highest instance is in the 18–30 year old age group. A prior history of headache or a prior history of post lumbar puncture headache increases the risk of recurrent headache. The size and orientation of the needle is also important.

Treatment of post lumbar puncture headache is bed rest for mild cases. In severe cases, the tear in the dura may be repaired with an epidural blood patch.

Myelography

In this technique, a lumbar puncture is first performed to allow the insertion of a radio-opaque dye into the spinal CSF pathways, so that evidence of spinal cord or lumbar nerve root entrapment may be demonstrated. Although this technique has, to a large extent, been replaced by MRI techniques (see above, p 33), myelography is still being undertaken.

The risk factors for myelography therefore include those listed above for lumbar puncture, plus the added risk of the dye which is introduced. Currently, the contrast medias used are all water soluble, and the only rare complications that have been ascribed to these agents is the risk of seizure activity. This is in contradistinction to the previous oil based contrasting agents (particularly myodil), which had a potential to cause arachnoiditis – and which led to major class action.

Complications of lumbar puncture

Cranial neuropathies

Abnormalities of the III, IV, V, VI, VII and VIII cranial nerves have been reported following lumbar puncture. These are usually transient, thought to be due to a decreased CSF pressure within the brain, leading to a degree of traction on the nerve. Some 0.4% of patients report visual symptoms, including double vision, blurred vision, spots before their eyes, intolerance of light and visual scintillation, and, again, some 0.4% have auditory complaints, including dizziness, tinnitus, popping ears and loss of hearing. These events are usually associated with typical post lumbar puncture headache.

Double vision, due to VI nerve palsy, follows about 0.25% lumbar punctures or spinal anaesthetics, and can be unilateral or bilateral. The weakness occurs four to 14 days after the procedure and resolves over four to six weeks.

Nerve root irritation/low back pain

When performing a lumbar puncture, the patient often complains of transient electric shocks or pins and needles, and this indicates a degree of contact between the spinal needle and the sensory root. This is reported by 13% of patients. Occasionally, permanent sensory or motor loss can occur. Some 35% of patients complain of back ache lasting for several days following a lumbar puncture. Occasionally, this persists for many months.

Infections

Bacterial meningitis is a rare complication of a lumbar puncture; more common, though still rare, is discitis (infection of the disc *per se*) and local abscess formation.

Venous complications

A very rare complication of lumbar puncture is an intracranial subdural haematoma (see Chapter 3). This is usually seen in the context of typical post lumbar puncture headache. The haematoma can be unilateral or bilateral and can be diagnosed anytime from three days to several months after the lumbar puncture. The mechanism is again thought to be low CSF pressure, resulting in traction on the blood vessel and tearing of the dural blood vessels. A subdural haematoma should be suspected when post lumbar puncture headache lasts for more than one week, or the headache recurs after a headache free interval and the headache does not have a postural component.

A traumatic lumbar puncture, where, through needle injuries, blood occurs in the CSF, occurs in about 75% of all diagnostic lumbar punctures and is not associated with severe sequelae.

Paraspinal haematomas are another rare complication, which present as severe low back pain or radicular pain, followed within hours or days by progressive paraparesis and evidence of cord compression.

BIOPSIES

Under well defined conditions, biopsies of nerve, muscle and brain may be indicated. These are, essentially, techniques which are the province of specialist neuroscience centres, and which are only undertaken when other modalities of investigation have failed to provide a diagnosis.

Muscle biopsy may be taken by a direct surgical approach or by a percutaneous biopsy. This permits the affected muscle to be examined histochemically and aids in the diagnosis of inherited neuromuscular disorders and of inflammatory muscle disorders (see Chapter 13).

A nerve biopsy has to be taken from a sensory nerve, so that, at most, the patient will be left with an area of absent sensation. Thus the terminal branch of the radial nerve in the upper limbs or the sural nerve in the lower limb are commonly biopsied. Such biopsies allow the differentiation of demyelinating and axonal neuropathies, and may show abnormal substances within the nerve (see Chapter 12).

Brain biopsy is usually undertaken for cerebral tumour to identify the type of tumour and to ensure that the mass lesion seen within the brain is not an abscess.

NEUROPSYCHOLOGY

In the same way that disorders of neurological function may be identified by examination and investigation, similarly, disorders of higher cerebral function are amenable to formal testing. This is the province of the clinical neuropsychologist. Although the neurologist will have a working knowledge of disorders of higher cerebral function, their formal assessment against normative values (for example, age, educational background) requires a much more sophisticated approach to the patient.

Cognitive functions are amenable to definition and measurement; thus the neuropsychologist is able to identify cognitive defects and to measure the deficit, the focus being on the severity of the effect on the patient's overall function, and how they correlate with what is known about the underlying pathology.

A detailed discussion of the techniques of neuropsychology is outside the remit of this book. However, neuropsychological investigation is of particular importance following brain injury which is either traumatic, iatrogenic or metabolic.

CHAPTER 3

HEAD INJURY

INTRODUCTION

Head injury is an important problem, in that deaths from head injury comprise 1–2% of all deaths from all causes, while some one third to one half of deaths due to trauma are due to head injury.

In a study of 174,160 patients, those with head injury comprised 34% of all cases, but resulted in 62% of deaths. There is a three times higher mortality in patients with head injury than in those without. Of those surviving, those with a head injury were substantially more impaired than those without. The former are therefore an important cause of morbidity.

The process of head injury can be separated into four phases. The primary injury, the delayed consequences of the primary injury, the secondary or additional injury and the recovery and functional outcome.

The primary injury is influenced by factors such as age, pre-existing disease, psychosocial status and nutritional status, sedatives, psychoactive, recreational and prescribed or proscribed drugs. The changes that occur in the brain cells themselves lead to the delayed consequences of the primary injury. It is this cellular dysfunction, which occurs as a consequence of the injury, which defines the nature and extent of the primary injury.

Secondary injury may result from fractures, reduced blood flow (ischaemia), raised intracranial pressure (ICP), seizures, infection and cerebral oedema.

Recovery and functional outcome are the products, therefore, of the primary injuries and its delayed consequences, the secondary injury and the care and rehabilitation that can be achieved.

TYPE OF HEAD INJURY

Head injuries may be divided into those which are closed and those which are penetrating.

A closed, or non-penetrating, head injury is one in which the impact accelerates or decelerates the head and in which there is no penetration of the skull by a foreign body, nor is there a fracture of bone driven inwards to deform or penetrate the brain. These injuries are usually caused by blunt objects or flat surfaces.

Penetrating injuries, on the other hand, by definition enter the brain and cause significant local deformation of the brain. They result from sharp or angular objects or missiles. The energy from these agents is locally dissipated within the brain, causing localised brain injury, in contradistinction to closed injuries, where there is generalised dissipation in the energy from the blow, leading to generalised brain injury.

In some instances of depressed fracture, there is a much less clear cut distinction than indicated above, since the blow may be of sufficient force to lead to a generalised dissipation of energy with a super-added local dissipation of energy, for example, a depressed fracture.

CLINICAL FEATURES

Head injuries in general may be classified as mild, moderate or severe. In a mild head injury, there are short periods of unconsciousness or amnesia, these being less than 12 hours. In a moderate head injury, there is the presence of a skull fracture or 13–24 hours of unconsciousness or post traumatic amnesia. In the severe head injury, there is evidence of brain contusion, intracerebral and intracranial haematoma, or more than 24 hours of unconsciousness and/or amnesia.

Retrograde amnesia is defined as the loss of memory of the events leading up to the injury in question. This is usually of short duration (up to an hour), but may occasionally be very much longer. The duration of retrograde amnesia, however, is not helpful in predicting the outcome or the severity of late neurological complications, in marked contradistinction to post traumatic amnesia. It is not uncommon for the duration of retrograde amnesia to 'shrink' with the passage of time. Hence, it is not uncommon to find that expert reports, undertaken a year apart, give a different estimate of the duration of retrograde amnesia. Retrograde amnesia never extends with the passage of time.

Post traumatic amnesia (PTA) is defined as the period from the impact until the patient is in continuous memory, and differs greatly from the period of unconsciousness. The duration of PTA has a major influence on the neurological sequelae, in that longer periods of post traumatic amnesia are, in general, associated with more severe injuries.

In a severe head injury, it is often difficult to estimate the duration of post traumatic amnesia. By the time the memory has returned continuously, the patient is usually in rehabilitation and no longer receiving as intensive a degree of nursing care as they did in the initial part of the trauma; hence, it is often the family who can give a better estimate of the duration of the PTA. This point may be semantic, in that any duration over 24 hours is, by definition, severe.

MANAGEMENT OF HEAD INJURY

Following head injury, the first point of contact is likely to be the ambulance service and then the casualty department. Crucial decisions have to be made as to the management of an individual with head injury, particularly when the situation may be clouded by alcohol or drug excess.

Bullock and Teasdale, in 'Surgical management of traumatic intracranial haematomas', in Bruyn, Kalawans and Vinken, *Handbook of Clinical Neurology*, 1990, pp 249–58, have set out the situations for undertaking a skull X-ray after a recent head injury:

(a) loss of consciousness or amnesia;

(b) neurological signs or symptoms;

(c) cerebrospinal fluid or blood from the nose or ear;

(d) suspected penetrating injury;

(e) scalp bruising or swelling; and

(f) difficulty in assessing the patient (that is, alcohol intoxication, epilepsy, children).

Further management has again been identified by the same authors, who produced a management algorithm for head injured patients at district general hospitals which have a CT scanner. They suggested that the fully conscious patient, with no history of any loss of consciousness, does not require a skull X-ray and could be observed at home. The patient presenting fully conscious with no past history of unconsciousness and having a skull X-ray which is negative can, again, can be observed at home.

Patients who present fully conscious, but have an abnormality on their skull X-ray, or patients who present with impaired consciousness or neurological signs, require an urgent CT scan. If negative, this should lead to observation in hospital until the patient is fully conscious, and then further observation at home.

If the scan is positive, or if the patient presents in a coma or with deteriorating consciousness, the patient needs to be resuscitated and transferred urgently to a neurosurgical unit. These guidelines are widely accepted.

The Glasgow coma scale (GCS) is now almost universally applied to patients with head injury. The maximum score is 15. Responses are measured and graded as follows:

Eye opening responses

Spontaneous	4
Speech	3
Painful stimulus	2
None	1

Motor responses in upper limbs

Obeys commands	6
Localises	5
Withdrawal	4 (normal flexion
Flexes abnormally	3 (spastic flexion)
Extends	2
None	1

} To pain

Verbal responses

Orientated	5
Confused	4
Inappropriate words	3
Incomprehensible sounds	2
None	1

The lower the GCS, the more severe the level of head injury.

MINOR HEAD INJURY

This is the commonest form of head injury encountered, equating to a GCS of 13–15. In various published series, these account for between 60% and 85% of all head injuries. More males suffer minor head injuries than females at all ages, and the peak rate for males is between the ages of 15 and 24.

In one large study, based on the assessment of over 3,000 patients, 42% were involved in a motor vehicle accident, of which occupants of a vehicle accounted for 64%, motor cyclists for 20%, pedestrians for 10%, and bicyclists for 6%. Falls accounted for 23% of the cases and assaults for 14%. Bicycle accidents not involving a motor vehicle, and sports and recreation activities both accounted for 6%. The remaining 9% included a wide variety of occasional events.

Following minor head injury, there is small, but definable, risk of patients having a serious neurological complication – the patients who talk and die. These are patients with a history of a minor head injury who, on initial presentation, appear to be relatively normal, but subsequently go on to develop either a subdural haematoma or raised intracranial pressure. Various studies have indicated a risk of between 1% and 3%, and virtually all of these patients have a GCS of 13 or 14 at the time of the first presentation.

The symptoms complained of by patients with minor head injury fall into three groups: the acute group, who present immediately after the injury and who are symptomatic for a period of a few days through to two or three weeks; the middle group, where the patients have the symptoms as for the acute group, and continue to have symptoms for several months; and the late group, where symptoms persist for longer than 12 months.

The acute group accounts for the vast majority of patients, and they complain of headache, nausea and general malaise. They usually complain of dizziness, which is rarely true rotational vertigo related to movement (see above, p 25); there is usually a more non-specific description of movement. They tend to be irritable and be sensitive to light and noise. They describe an inability to concentrate, with memory impairment and lack of insight, and describe fatigue and the need for long hours of sleep. These symptoms usually clear rapidly after the event.

In the relatively small group of patients in the middle group, these symptoms persist and then gradually emerge into behavioural changes with bad temper, irritability and sensitivity of light and noise. Family and social relationships deteriorate, and insight is poor. They report impairment of cognitive function with poor concentration and memory, slow responses and failure to cope at work. They report fatigue which comes on after a predictable period of activity, and which accumulates rapidly if activity continues. All their other symptoms are magnified by the fatigue, yet they have insomnia. They complain of headache due to scalp and neck injury and also stress; in reaction to their symptoms, they develop forms of depression and anger.

The late group is an even smaller group of patients, who remain symptomatic for longer than 12 months.

Treatment is rarely required for the acute group. In the middle group, assessment by a neurologist and a neuropsychologist is important to exclude any other cause for their symptoms and usually, with appropriate neuropsychological treatment, the patients settle completely. The late stage requires, in addition to neurological and neuropsychological input, psychiatric input.

The existence of an acute post concussional syndrome is rarely disputed and various published series account for between 80% and 90% of all minor head injury patients.

The validity of the long term syndromes has been the subject of considerable debate. It has been argued that neuropsychometric tests in such long term symptomatic individuals show defects in attention span and in concentration and memory. However, others have argued that these abnormalities relate to concomitant anxiety. Pearce, in 'Post traumatic syndrome and whiplash injuries', 1995, makes the following cogent observation:

> The quality of recovery depends on many factors. The most important are age and the victim's pre-injury personality, job, motivation and resilience. Another adverse factor is insecure medical reassurance soon after the injury which determines the patient's fears of brain damage and can delay return to work. Alcoholism, previous head injury and multiple injuries worsen the outcome ... Sadly more suggestible or manipulative plaintiffs in time come to believe the sick role they have chosen to adopt and they remain tragically, but unnecessarily, crippled for life.

Arguments over the long term sequelae of minor head injury will continue and the issue, at present, remains unresolved.

There are a small group of patients who, following a minor head injury, develop true rotational vertigo, which is modified by posture. These patients can be shown to have an abnormality predominantly of the labyrinth, although occasionally labyrinthine pathways may be involved. One in five patients who is appropriately questioned and investigated will describe postural vertigo. This commonly settles within 12–24 months following the head injury, but some 10% of those suffering from vestibular dysfunction will have persistent symptoms after 24 months, the persistence of symptoms being independent of litigation. For discussion of the relationship between minor head injury and migraine, see Chapter 9.

MODERATE AND SEVERE HEAD INJURY

Although these two groups of head injury patients form only a small proportion of all head injuries, their neurological sequelae are amongst the most devastating. Given that the majority of head injuries occur in late adolescent and early adult life, normally functioning young people may sustain horrendous neurological deficit which renders them dependent on others for the rest of their life.

In blunt head injury, there will almost certainly be a laceration to the scalp at the time of the head injury, and such lesions are good indicators of the site of impact. The presence of a skull fracture (Figure 3.1) indicates that the impact had considerable force. However, many patients who have a skull fracture make complete recovery without any evidence of neurological deficit. In patients with moderate to severe head injuries, where there is impairment of consciousness, the risk of developing a haematoma in the presence of a skull fracture is approximately one in four.

Figure 3.1   **Skull X-ray showing linear fracture running from the region of the temple to the parietal bone**

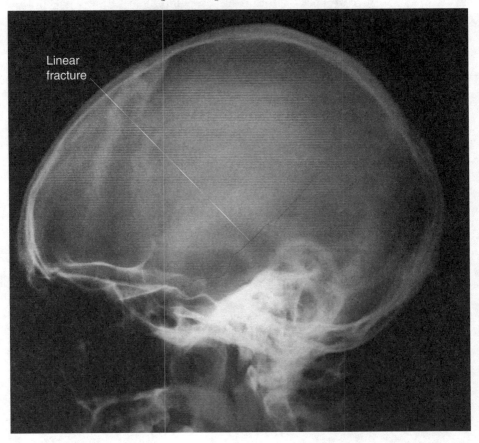

Linear
fracture

A fracture may be depressed (Figure 3.2a and b), that is, the fragments of the inner table of the skull are depressed by at least the thickness of the skull. A depressed fracture is said to be compound; if there is an associated laceration of the scalp, and a penetrating or open injury, there is also a tear to the dura.

Fractures to the base of the skull are again evidence of a severe impact. They often pass through the middle ear or the anterior cranial fossa, leading to cerebrospinal fluid otorrhea (leakage of CSF from the ear), or CSF rhinorrhea (leakage of CSF through the nose), or damage to the cranial nerves, particularly I, II, VII and VIII.

Figure 3.2a   Skull X-ray, with depressed fracture shown only as increased density

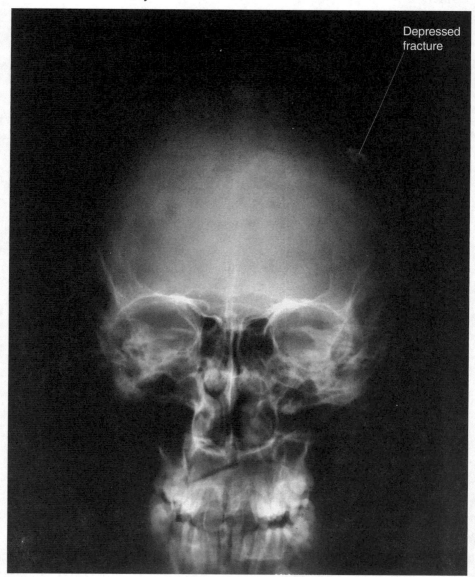

Depressed
fracture

Figure 3.2b CT scan of the same fracture, showing the greater clarity with which CT identifies depressed fractures

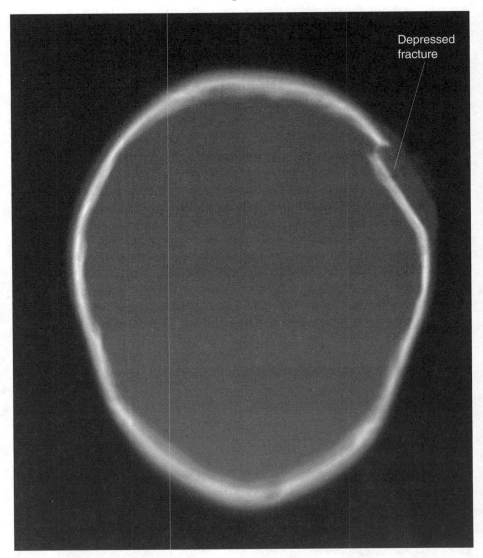

Depressed fracture

Contusions and lacerations of the brain are common following blunt head injury (Figure 3.3). Contusions occur as a result of tearing of the small blood vessels overlying the brain and thus occur on the surface of the brain. They are usually seen on the tops of gyri, but occasionally can be found over the deep fissures.

Figure 3.3   **CT scan of the brain, showing multiple contusions in the frontal lobes and temporal lobes**

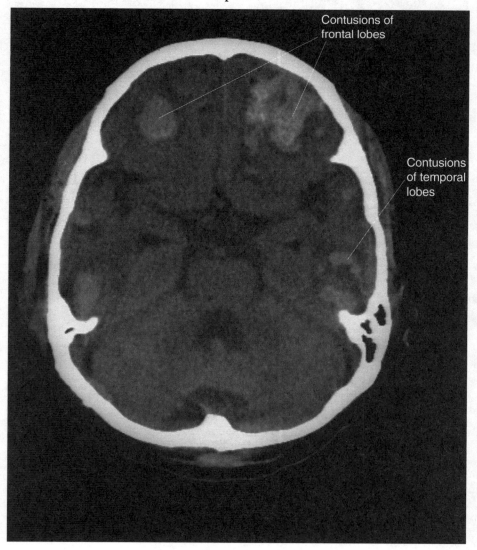

Contusions of frontal lobes

Contusions of temporal lobes

The brain is capable of movement within the rigid skull and is fixed anteriorly by the olfactory nerve. In blunt injury to the skull, the brain can be thrown forward or backward. In forward movement, the frontal lobes and the anterior part of the temporal lobes will show contusion. In backward movement, the occipital lobes will show contusion, and in the backward movement there is a risk of the olfactory nerve shearing; hence, trauma on the occiput will produce a coup lesion in the occiput and can produce a contra coup lesion in the frontal or temporal lobes.

Intracranial haemorrhage is seen in the severest varieties of blunt head injury and can occur in about 55% of patients. These haemorrhages, as noted previously with respect to minor head injury, are the commonest cause of clinical deterioration and death in patients who have had a lucid interval following their head injury. The haemorrhages may be extradural, subdural or intracerebral (Figure 3.4a, b, c and d).

Figure 3.4a **CT scan of the brain, showing an acute right extradural haematoma, with brain compression**

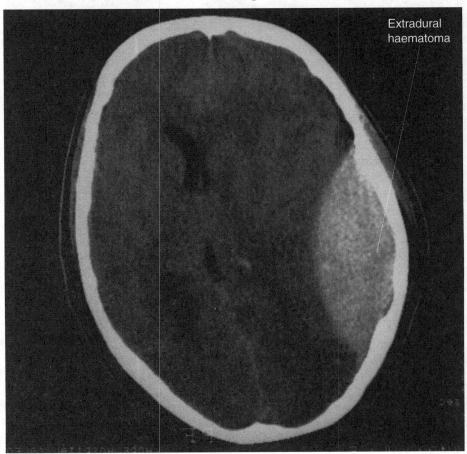

Extradural haematoma is a consequence of bleeding from the meningeal vessels, and is outside the dura. The bleeding, therefore, strips the dura from the skull and causes progressive indentation and flattening of the brain. Usually, extradural haematomata occur as a result of a tear in the middle meningeal artery in relation to fractures of the temporal bone, one of the thinnest parts of the skull, but they may occur, in 20% of cases, in the frontal or parietal areas, or occasionally in the posterior fossa.

Subdural haematomata are very acute. In this instance, the bleeding occurs under the dura, and hence the blood can spread freely through the subdural space and cover the entire hemisphere of the skull. Acute haematomata

Figure 3.4b CT scan of the brain, showing an acute left subdural haematoma

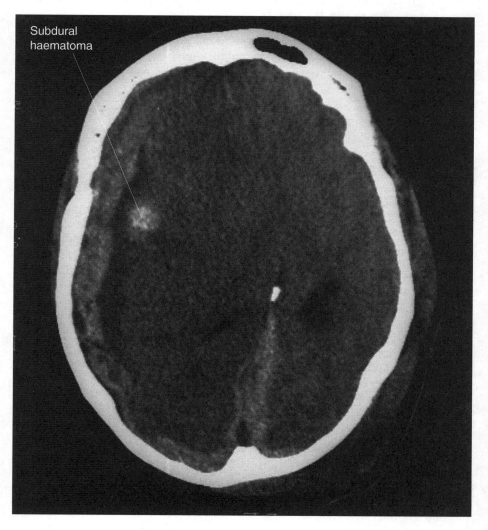

Subdural haematoma

develop rapidly over a period of several hours. A haematoma is defined as acute only if composed of clots of blood, as subacute when it is composed of a combination of clotted and fluid blood, and as chronic when the haematoma is fluid. In severely head injured patients, these would be identified by appropriate imaging techniques and would be treated appropriately.

Chronic subdural haematoma may present weeks or months after a head injury, particularly in the elderly. In this instance, often a trivial head injury is identified in between 20% and 50% of cases. In the remaining individuals, no precipitating cause can be found.

Figure 3.4c   MR scan of the brain, showing mid line subdural haemorrhage

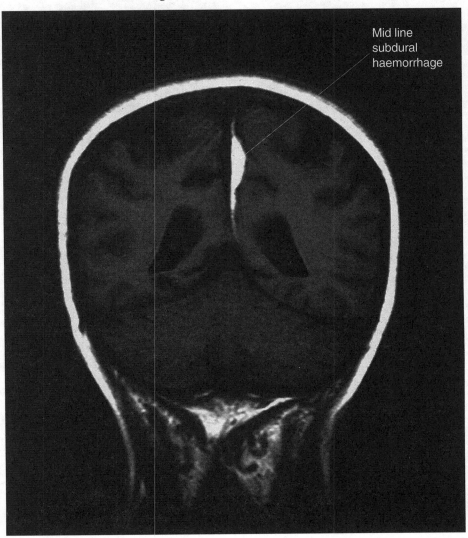

Mid line subdural haemorrhage

Intracerebral haematomas are caused by direct rupture of the intrinsic cerebral blood vessels, and are most commonly found in the frontal and temporal regions. They usually develop in the same areas as contusions and their appearance can be delayed by 48 hours, or even up to a week, from the original injury.

Figure 3.4d   **MR scan of the brain, showing large right cerebellar intrahemispheric (intracerebral) haematoma**

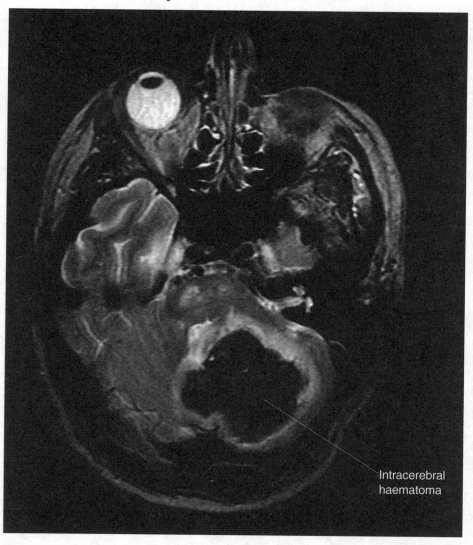

Intracerebral haematoma

All of the factors mentioned above can contribute to the development of raised intracranial pressure and, hence, most severely brain damaged individuals have their intracranial pressure monitored by direct pressure recording. The importance of this is underlined by the fact that raised intracranial pressure itself can cause severe neurological damage. As the pressure in the super tentorial portion increases, this can cause distortion of the brain stem, and secondary infarction or haemorrhage within the brain stem. The long term consequences of the latter may be more significant than the former.

In patients with a fracture, there is also a high risk of infection.

In addition to these focal abnormalities which can occur within the brain, it is now recognised that diffuse axonal injury (DAI) is a very common concomitant of severe head injury.The concept was based on pathological examination of brains which showed that the major damage was occurring in the white matter and within the axons. It was thought that this was due to a combination of sheering factors, ischaemic damage and cerebral oedema, as a consequence of intracranial expanding lesions. In patients who survive the head injury who have evidence of DAI, there is usually severe and profound handicap.

MISSILE HEAD INJURY

These are much less common than blunt head injury. They are classified as depressed, penetrating or perforating.

In the depressed injury, the missile does not enter the cranial cavity, but produces a depressed fracture of the skull. The resulting brain damage is local to the area of depression.

In penetrating injuries, the object enters the skull, but does not pass through it. Small or sharp objects, for example, a nail, may produce very little injury to the skull or the brain. Patients with, for example, a knife or a screwdriver penetrating the skull and brain may not have had any loss of consciousness. These patients carry a very high risk of the development of infection.

Perforating injuries, when the missile punctures the skull and exits on the other side, are usually due to a bullet. In most cases, these are rapidly fatal.

The relationship between epilepsy and head injury is discussed in Chapter 5.

OUTCOME FOLLOWING MODERATE TO SEVERE HEAD INJURY

Not infrequently, patients with moderate or severe head injury have major systemic disturbances associated with autonomic abnormalities, including abnormalities of respiration, cardiac arrhythmias, hypotension and temperature disturbances. In many of these cases, extracranial injuries and complications affect these functions and they are not a useful predictor of outcome. Age is predictive of outcome, in that increasing age is associated with an increase in severe outcome.

The Glasgow coma scale 24 hours after the onset of coma can be used as a predictor of outcome. Of patients whose total GCS is three or four, 87% will not survive, or will be left in a persistent vegetative state, and only 7% would be left with moderate disability or good recovery.

Of patients who showed a GCS of five, six or seven, some 53% will either die, or be in a persistent vegetative state, whereas 34% will make a moderate or good recovery.

Of patients with a GCS of eight, nine or 10 at 24 hours, 27% will die, or be in a persistent vegetative state, whereas 68% will make a moderate or good recovery, and of patients who have a GCS of more than 11, only 12% will die, or be in a persistent vegetative state, whereas 87% will make a moderate or good recovery.

The Glasgow outcome scale (GOS) has been derived from these measurements and comprises five categories. The first of these is death. The second is a persistent vegetative state, where patients may exhibit cycles of sleeping and waking with eye opening, but are unresponsive to commands, are speechless, and show no evidence of cognitive interaction with their environment.

Category three is defined as severe disability. Such patients are dependent on others for daily support because of neuropsychological or physical disability. Severely disabled patients may be institutionalised.

Category four represents moderate disability, that is, patients who are independent to a degree. These patients can utilise public transport, do not require a sheltered environment, and are more or less independent performing daily activities. They may, however, have residual disabilities such as hemiparesis, aphasia, impairment of memory and cognition and alterations of personality.

Category five is defined as good recovery. These patients resume a normal lifestyle, despite the possibility of behavioural neuropyscho-physical sequelae. The assessment of such patients from the medico-legal standpoint requires the input of a neurologist or a neurosurgeon to define the level of clinical disability, and this needs to be supplemented by up to date magnetic resonance imaging of the brain and, in patients with epilepsy or potential for epilepsy, electroencephalogram assessment. Their intellectual functioning has to established by a neuropsychologist. This involves not only assessment of intellectual ability, but also detailed assessment of frontal lobe functioning. Occupational and physiotherapy reports are also needed, so that the total caring needs of the individual can be assessed.

CHAPTER 4

SPINAL INJURY

INTRODUCTION

The spine is composed of four segments: the cervical, thoracic, lumbar and sacral. There are seven cervical vertebrae, 12 thoracic vertebrae and five lumbar vertebrae. The sacral vertebrae fuse together in a single bony mass.

In the caudal direction (from the head to the bottom of the lumbar spine), the vertebral bodies increase in size and becoming increasingly specialised for weight bearing, whereas the cervical spine is the most mobile area of the vertebral column. In addition to its role in maintaining stability, the vertebral column provides protection for the spinal cord and it associated nerve roots.

The individual vertebrae are composed of a body, the pedicles, the facet joints and the lamina (Figure 4.1). These bound the spinal canal. Contained within the canal is the spinal cord and the exiting nerve roots.

Figure 4.1   Structure of individual vertebrae

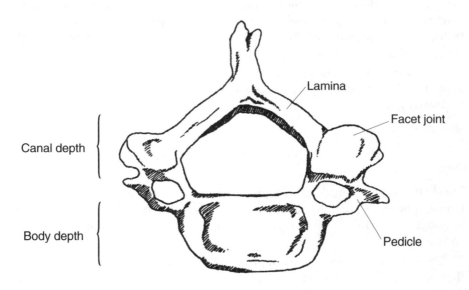

The contour of the cervical canal is subject to variation, its average diameter being 16–17 mm, ranging from a narrow canal at 11 mm to a wide canal at 20–21 mm. Variation may be developmental or due to disease process. Consequent upon the shape and contour of the spinal canal, are the shape and contour of the exiting foramina, through which the nerves destined for the arms and legs have to pass. Hence, abnormalities in foraminal diameter may also be due to developmental factors or disease processes.

The discs lie between the individual vertebrae. Their function is to maintain the interspace width, while strongly binding together the opposing vertebral surfaces in a way that permits small degrees of painless motion. The disc is bound in place by the annulus fibrosis. The interlacing nature of the annulus implies that in rotation some fibres are under tension while others are relaxed.

The individual vertebrae are bound together by a series of ligaments which are uniaxial in nature and hence are designed to carry loads primarily in one direction only, that is, the direction in which the fibres are running. They may be compared to an elastic band in that they resist tensile forces but when subject to compression they tend to buckle. These ligaments have two important functions. First, they give strength and stability to the complex articulations of the spine and, secondly, they act to protect the spine and its contents against excessive forces; because of their strength and viscoelastic properties they are able to absorb great amounts of energy.

Within the spinal column, the cervical spine is unique, in that it has to carry out a wide range of movement and yet protect the underlying spinal cord and nerve roots, and the combination of safety and free range of motion in the cervical segment of the spinal column is largely dependent upon the integrity of the ligaments.

Spinal cord injury can therefore accrue as a consequence of trauma in a spine which is normal, which is developmentally abnormal or abnormal due to disease process.

SPINAL CORD INJURY

This is the most severe form of injury which can occur. In common with head injury, it is more likely to affect males than females, by a factor of four, and, although occurring in all age groups, it is commonest in the late teens and early 20's.

The commonest spinal cord injuries follow motor vehicle accidents (48%), then falls (21%), sports injuries (13%), and other acts of violence (15%); the remaining 3% are accounted for by miscellaneous rare events.

The presentation is always that of loss of sensation and loss of function beneath the level of the spinal cord injury. This is relatively easily determined by neurological examination. Plain radiographic examination indicates the level of the bony abnormality and magnetic resonance techniques indicate the level of damage to the spinal cord as well as the surrounding tissues.

In the acute phase of management of patients with spinal injury, there is now evidence that intravenous methylprednisolone given within eight hours of the injury can influence and improve the outcome. The prognosis for recovery is best in those who have an incomplete spinal lesion, and also in patients in whom there is evidence of some return of motor or sensory function within 48 hours of the injury.

If it appears that no function has returned after three months following the injury, then it is unlikely that further recovery will take place. If there has been some recovery in three months, then a further 18 months should elapse before a final assessment is made. However, the higher the lesion in the spinal column, the greater the degree of neurological dysfunction.

Injury at lumbar level

In lesions below L4, L5, S1 and S2, the spinal cord is not involved, and the predominant problem is interference with nerve supply to the bowel and to the bladder. Sexual function may also be affected.

With lesions at L4 downwards, the degree of weakness that results is dependent upon the level of the lesion. Affectation of the lower roots only will lead to weakness of the foot; at mid level, this will lead to weakness of the knee; and at the highest level, weakness of the hip will occur. These can usually be overcome by arthoses and walking aids, and it is rare for patients to require a wheelchair.

At the L1/2/3 level, the major change is in bladder function, where there tends to be over activity in the nerves controlling the bladder and the bowel, rather than under activity as at the lower levels. The motor problems are similar to those at L4 downwards.

Injury at thoracic level

Injury between T7 and T12 indicates that the spinal cord is now involved, making it probable that the patient will require a wheelchair for mobility. Normally, transfers, eating, dressing and personal hygiene are easily achieved. The higher levels, towards T7, imply that the muscles of respiration are involved and, in such a situation, chest infections are more likely to occur.

The bladder and bowel function is similar to that described at L1/2/3, with hyperexcitability, which usually means that drainage devices are not required.

At levels T1 to T6, wheelchairs remain the only mode of ambulation and, although achievable, transfers, dressing and attention to personal hygiene require great training and persistence. The degree of bladder dysfunction usually requires an indwelling device.

Injury at cervical level

At C7 and C8 levels, the hands are involved, and the patient's ability is significantly limited. There will usually be great difficulty with grip, although shoulder and upper arm movement is preserved. Wheelchair modifications are often required because of the impaired grip. Dressing and personal hygiene may require help, and adaptations for bathroom systems are required. Because of the involvement of the muscles of respiration, chest infections are a recurrent problem. Lesions at C7/8 are the highest level at which an individual can survive without a permanent carer, although this is not achieved by all individuals.

At the C6 level, considerably more upper limb function is lost, and to use the limbs for eating requires adaptations. It is still possible to use a manually operated wheelchair, but most patients prefer electrically operated wheelchairs. Dressing and personal hygiene usually require an attendant, as do transfers.

At the C5 level, the patient has shoulder and elbow function but no wrist or hand function. Eating becomes increasingly difficult, and transfers, dressing and personal hygiene are impossible without a carer.

Patients with C1/2/3, and many patients with C4, lesions require artificial ventilation with a portable respiratory attached to the wheelchair. Most patients require permanent tracheostomy, and clearly require full time care.

SPINAL SPONDYLOSIS AND DISC DISEASE

Cervical spine disc disease

Cervical spondylosis and/or disc protrusion may present as a radiculopathy (pain and paraesthesiae in the distribution of a single nerve root in the arm), myelopathy (involvement of the spinal cord) or a combination of both (myeloradiculopathy). In a young individual, an acute presentation most likely indicates a disc protrusion.

The classical history in a radiculopathy is a stepwise progression of neck pain to shoulder pain, then pain in the arm, with paraesthesiae and subsequently weakness. The mean age of acute disc prolapse in young people (that is, those under 50 years of age) is 37, and the most commonly affected roots are C6/7, accounting for 54%, and C5/6, accounting for 35%. Prolapses at C4/5 and C7 to T1 account for 6% each. Cervical disc prolapses are about 1/10th as common as lumbar disc prolapse. Only 20% of patients will give a history of antecedent trauma.

Spondylotic disease increases significantly with age, being present in 50% of normal individuals by the age of 50, and 90% by the age of 65. It should be noted that spondylosis is a degenerative process due to the interplay of numerous factors, which results in disc dehydration, loss of disc height, disc protrusion and the formation of bony osteophytes which may encroach not only on the exiting foramina, but also on the spinal canal. There is no evidence to suggest that this is an active inflammatory process as in arthritis.

Cervical spondylosis usually involves two adjacent levels and approximately 60% of cases occur at C5 and C6 (Figure 4.2a, b and c). The mean age of presentation is 59 years. The usual presenting symptom is neck pain with restriction of neck movement, referred pain to the shoulder, which is often exacerbated by carrying in the affected arm (brachialgia), with pain at the back of the neck extending to the head, which may become an encircling band. Patients are typically more symptomatic first thing in the morning, with a recurrence of their symptoms towards the end of the day.

Figure 4.2a   MR scan of cervical spine, showing mid cervical spondylosis

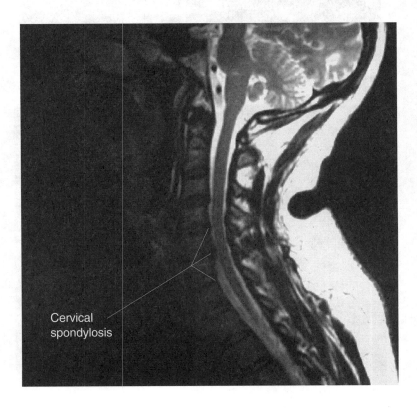

Cervical spondylosis

Figure 4.2b   Normal MR of cervical spine

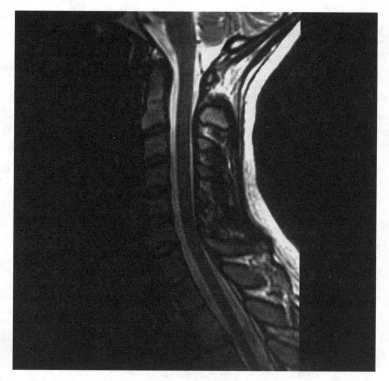

Figure 4.2c   Normal MR of cervical spine

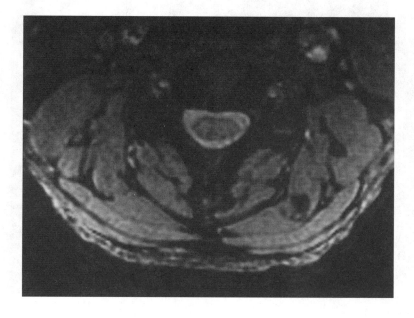

When pain extends beyond the level of the shoulder into the distribution of a nerve root, it is then frequently accompanied by paraesthesiae and demonstrable neurological abnormalities in the upper limbs, comprising suppression or absence of reflexes and objective loss of sensation. Most acute attacks of cervical radiculopathy resolve with time, particularly when aided by appropriate physiotherapy techniques.

Those patients who do not resolve, and go on to develop a chronic syndrome, with intermittent dull aching discomfort and clear cut signs of dermatomal sensory abnormality, reflex changes and muscle wasting, may well be amenable to surgery (see below, p 74).

Cervical spondylotic myelopathy indicates that the spinal cord is involved (Figure 4.3). Symptoms develop gradually, often over years, but can be precipitated by injury or trauma to an underlying abnormal canal. Initial complaints are usually those of difficulty in walking, with aching pain in the lower limbs increased by exercise and relieved by rest. Abnormal sensations in the lower limb often comprise band like constrictions, or a sensation of diffuse pins and needles or fluid trickling over the leg. Disturbance of bladder function is a late occurrence.

Figure 4.3   **MR scan of cervical spine showing cervical spondylosis with cord compression (cervical myelopathy)**

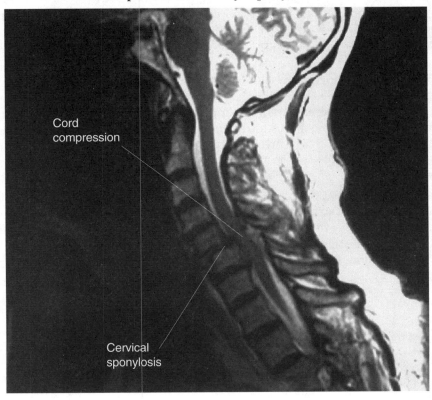

The progression of the motor involvement of the lower limbs is one of increasing spasticity, which further limits the walking ability, and the patient often complains of profound fatigue occurring after limited exercise. With further progression, the legs have a tendency to jerk involuntarily with rest following exercise or in bed at night, and they tremble spontaneously (clonus).

Myeloradiculopathy combines the symptoms of a radiculopathy with cord involvement. The syndrome is usually one of intermittent progression. However, acute presentations can follow a hyper-extension injury to the spondylotic canal (see below, p 76).

Patients with narrow cervical canal diameters are at greatest risk of the development of myelopathic symptoms. In flexion and extension of the neck, the volume of the cervical canal is reduced by some 25%. If 33% of the canal is already occupied by spondylotic disease and/or disc protrusion, a further reduction of 25% would be of significance in a narrow diameter canal, but of less significance in a wide diameter canal.

Most patients presenting with myelopathy or myeloradiculopathy will be offered surgical intervention. Surgery for acute disc prolapses, via either the anterior or posterior approach, is usually successful, with more than 85% of patients reporting a greater than 98% reduction in symptomatology at follow up of more than 10 years. Surgery for spondylotic radiculopathy does not yield such good results, which may reflect the potentially increasing age of the population. However, between 65% and 75% of patients, at follow up of greater than five years, report significant (greater than 75%) relief of their symptomatology.

In contradistinction to the results obtained for acute disc prolapse and radiculopathy, the results of surgery for myelopathy and myeloradiculopathy are significantly worse. Overall, it appears that a third of patients have some degree of improvement, a third stop deteriorating and a third continue to deteriorate. In all cases of myelopathy, medical management (with antispastic agents and attention to the neurogenic bladder) must complement surgical intervention.

The anterior approach (Cloward's operation), when associated with a fusion, throws extra strain on the discs above and below the level of the fusion. There is increasing evidence that this leads to acceleration of degenerative disease processes at these levels, and these changes are frequently symptomatic.

Thoracic spine disc disease

Most thoracic disc prolapses occur between T8 and T11, and account for about 1% of all spinal disc prolapses. If the disc prolapses laterally, then the intercostal nerves are involved and the patient develops radicular pain, coming round from the back, through the flank and into the abdomen.

If the disc prolapses centrally, then a myelopathy develops. As with cervical myelopathy, the results of surgery for thoracic myelopathy are disappointing.

Lumbar spine disc disease

Back pain, with or without sciatica, is one of the most common complaints presented to general practitioners. Lumbar spondylosis encompasses the same range of disease processes as within the cervical spine, with osteophyte formation, disc degeneration and hypertrophy of the lamina.

About 50% of people in light manual work will experience back pain and some 65% of patients involved in heavy manual work will likewise complain of back pain.

Approximately 80% of the population will have significant low back pain at some point and, of these, some 35% will develop sciatica. This is most common in the 30–50 year age range, and most lumbar disc herniations involve L4/5 and L5/S1 (Figure 4.4). The usual complaint is of back pain,

Figure 4.4   **MR scan of spine, showing acute L4/5 lumbar disc prolapse**

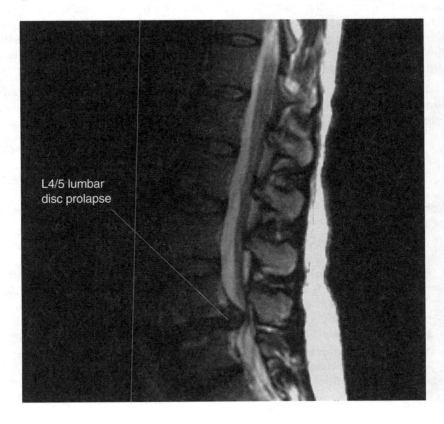

L4/5 lumbar
disc prolapse

followed by radicular pain in the lower limb, followed by paraesthesiae in the same distribution, and then leg weakness. Bladder involvement is rare. Although the majority of patients complain of sensory disturbance, objective sensory loss is only found in about 50% of patients. The deep tendon reflexes, particularly ankle reflexes, are usually absent.

Following the first episode of low back pain with sciatica, 66% of patients recover within one month, and 85% will be asymptomatic within three months. Approximately 25% of patients will give a history of trauma or exertion prior to their first episode of back pain and sciatica.

Those patients whose back pain and sciatica fails to settle with conservative measures, are usually offered surgery, either via an open laminectomy and discectomy, or using microdiscectomy techniques. Overall, up to 85% of patients consider the operation a success, and the majority of these (95%) return to work. Figures for spondylotic disease as opposed to acute disc prolapse are 75% and 78% respectively.

Patients with extensive spondylotic disease in the lumbar spine may develop lumbar canal stenosis. This presents as so called 'neurogenic claudication' in the lower limbs. In this situation, the patient will have pain on walking, which forces them to stop. In contradistinction to vascular claudication, where the pain clears within a matter of seconds, it can take between five and 15 minutes before the pain disappears. With time, the patient's walking distance shortens, and it takes longer for the pain to diminish. These patients show, on examination, 'hour glass' constrictions at multiple levels within the lumbar spine (Figure 4.5).

Surgical intervention is usually indicated for patients with lumbar canal stenosis. More than 60% of patients report relief from symptoms after surgical intervention.

WHIPLASH INJURIES

Pearce, in 'Post traumatic syndrome and whiplash injuries', in *Recent Advances in Clinical Neurology*, 1995, notes:

Few topics provoke so much controversy or heated opinion, based on so little fact, as whiplash injuries. In emergency departments, orthopaedic, neurological and rheumatology clinics, and not least in the courts, this common syndrome is shrouded in mystery and creates clinical insecurity in those who attempt to explain its mechanism, prognosis and treatment. These problems are compounded in medico-legal practice, where the potential rewards of successful litigation may colour the clinical picture.

Most victims of whiplash injury have however sustained no more than a minor sprain of the soft tissues and unusually severe or protracted complaints may demand explanations which lie, outside the field of organic and psychiatric illness.

Figure 4.5   MR scan of lumbar spine, showing significant lumbar canal stenosis, with a typical hourglass appearance

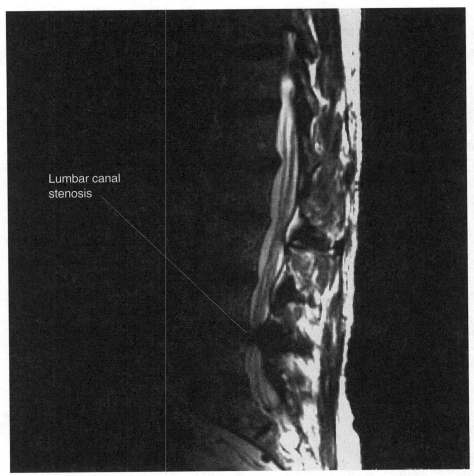

Lumbar canal
stenosis

This statement underlines the wide diversity of opinion in the field of neck injuries. It is instructive to note that the term 'whiplash' does not appear in the index to the *Oxford Textbook of Medicine*. Whiplash syndrome has become a short hand way of encompassing a wide variety of complaints whereas, in truth, the term implies only a mechanism of injury to a part of the spine.

Strictly speaking, whiplash should be reserved for hyperextension/flexion injuries of the spine sustained in a rear end shunt. However, by common usage, it now encompasses injuries to the cervical spine from side impact and front end collisions as well as rear end shunts.

In a hyperflexion/extension injury, there are four phases to the event. In the first phase, following a rear end impact, the torso is forced backwards into the seat and the head and neck initially remain fixed, while the vehicle moves forward underneath. Subsequently, the head and neck begin to extend.

In the second phase, the forces in the seat begin to return to normal, and this pushes the torso forwards at the same time as the head and neck are still moving backwards.

In the third phase, the torso has stopped moving forwards and the head and neck start their acceleration forward.

In the fourth phase, the head and neck have stopped moving forward and then the head snaps back, causing further extension.

It is highly improbable that an individual will be sitting in a perfectly vertically aligned position and, thus, virtually all so called hyperextension/ flexion injuries include an element of rotation, and it is this rotating force which underlies neurologic involvement in whiplash injury.

Neck pain develops in approximately 50% of patients involved in a front or side impact accident. This figure rises to about 85% in rear end collisions. In rear end collisions, the incidence of whiplash injuries decreases as the crash severity increases. One study has shown that the incidence of whiplash symptomatology occurs in about 80% of patients where the vehicle is drivable, compared to 66% of patients in which the vehicle has to be removed.

Wearing a seatbelt increases the risk of symptoms of whiplash injury from 50% to 75%. Although the provision of head restraints theoretically should reduce the risk of whiplash injuries by some 24%, it is rare for these to be properly adjusted, and incorrectly adjusted head restraints may in fact increase the severity of the injury.

Symptoms of neck pain following a whiplash injury are more common in females, particularly the 20–40 age group, by a ratio of 7:3.

Clinical course

The commonest complaints following a whiplash injury are neck pain, and headaches, dizziness and pins and needles. The neck pain occurs within six hours of the impact in 65% of patients, within 24 hours in a further 25% of patients, and within 72 hours in the remaining 10% of patients.

The pain is usually associated with restriction of neck movement, and is aggravated by neck movement. The majority of patients with neck pain will also describe headache, which in about 50% of patients is a continuation of the neck pain up into the back of the head. However, generalised headaches are seen in about 25% of patients, and at other locations in the remaining 25%. These headaches are often described as bursting or gripping. They are influenced by movement but not increased by coughing, stooping or straining, and have no associated visual disturbance. In a prospective study of patients with neck pain and headache only, approximately 35% were still symptomatic at three months, by six months this had fallen to 25%, and by 12 months, to 20%.

Complaints of dizziness occur in approximately 66% of patients, and are usually in the context of neck pain and headache. The patient usually complains of non specific dizziness, and true rotational vertigo, indicating disease of the labyrinth, is unusual.

Complaints of pins and needles (paraesthesiae) in the upper extremities are common after whiplash injury, and in one study 33% of patients complained of symptoms, but had no objective neurological dysfunction. Within this group, 33% still reported paraesthesiae at a follow up of 20 months. This group of patients has to be distinguished from those patients who have a radicular distribution of paraesthesiae or objective neurological dysfunction (see below). In a retrospective study of whiplash, at two years, 33% of patients were still symptomatic. However, the majority of the symptomatic patients had evidence of organic dysfunction.

Given the complexity of the arrangements of the bones, ligaments, joints and muscles around the neck, it is not surprising that patients develop neck pain, headache and non specific complaints of dizziness, following a wrenching injury to the neck. However, for the majority of patients this is a self-limiting condition. Pearce ('Post traumatic syndrome and whiplash injuries', 1995) has noted that 89% of patients are back to normal work by six months, but 18% of them still had discomfort or pain and took analgesics intermittently or regularly. At one year, the figures were 94% and 34% respectively, showing only a small further improvement.

There is evidence therefore that the so called 'uncomplicated whiplash injury' can be associated with persistent symptomatology in a small group of patients. However, closer examination of that group indicates that the majority fall into a category of patients who have had a whiplash injury and have had neurological signs and symptoms from the onset. It is important that this group of patients are identified as separate from the overall group of whiplash injury. These are patients who, following the injury, have a radicular distribution of sensory disturbance and pain in one or other upper limb, or patients in whom, after the initial injury has subsided, are aware of residual radicular symptomatology in an upper limb. These patients, on examination, are more likely to show objective neurological signs, and investigation, particularly with MR techniques, to show evidence of pre-existing spondylotic disease and/or disc prolapse.

In context, it is interesting to note that persistence of symptoms is greater in the older age group of patients compared to the younger age group, as would be expected from the evolution of degenerative cervical spondylosis with age.

Recent MR studies of the cervical spines of asymptomatic individuals have shown that disc degeneration is a common observation, being present in 17% of discs of men, and 12% of discs of women in their twenties, increasing to 86% and 89% respectively over the age of 60, with the rate of change being linear. Disc prolapse which had caused root and cord compression was seen in patients even though the patients were asymptomatic.

In such patients, the volume of the cervical canal and the exiting foramina would therefore be decreased, and, hence, a whiplash injury with neurological symptoms is likely to have converted a pre-existing asymptotic radiculopathy or myelopathy into a symptomatic condition.

Follow up studies of patients who have had a whiplash injury with a radiologically normal neck at the time of the whiplash have shown that approximately 40% go on to develop degenerative disc disease, compared to the expected incidence of 6% in those who did not have a whiplash. Similarly, long term follow up of patients who had pre-existing degenerative changes at the time of the whiplash, show that new degenerative changes occurred at a further level in 55% of those patients.

Other studies have shown that, in all ages, degenerative spondylosis was more common following whiplash injury, occurring in 33% of patients, as compared to 10% of controls, on a 10 year follow up. This suggest that there is evidence of advancement of the development of spondylotic disease in a previously normal neck, and exacerbation of the disease in a spondylotic neck, following whiplash.

The scalene muscles lie at the side of the neck, and are instrumental in supporting the neck. Emerging between the scalene muscles is the brachial plexus, and some of the so called diffuse paraesthesiae occurring after whiplash injury may relate to damage to the brachial plexus at the time of the whiplash.

Carpal tunnel syndrome following whiplash injury has been described. These are patients who have extended their wrist to brace against the steering wheel, and thus cause a traction injury to the median nerve. This usually clears spontaneously, without recourse to surgery.

Prognosis

The majority of patients who have long term disability following whiplash, do so as a consequence of involvement of the nervous system. The incidence is higher for those involved in rear end collisions, compared to those involved in front or side impact collisions, and higher in patients who have not braced themselves for the impact.

Treatment

Secondary gain, exaggeration and malingering have to be considered in all patients with a whiplash injury, although the evidence suggests that these psychological factors are responsible in only a minority of patients with persistent complaints. Current evidence suggests that most patients who are still symptomatic when litigation is completed are not cured by the verdict. The end of litigation does not signal the end of symptoms for many patients, except for the distinct minority who exaggerate or malinger.

The majority of patients with an uncomplicated whiplash (that is, one which does not have any involvement of the nervous system) respond to immobilisation of the neck in the first instance, with subsequent mobilisation by physiotherapy. With the majority of patients, symptoms settle over a period of two to 12 weeks.

In the case of patients in whom there is a neurological component to their symptoms (brachialgia, paraesthesiae, weakness, myelopathy), investigation is indicated prior to subsequent treatment, which ranges from physiotherapy through to surgery.

CHAPTER 5

COMA AND BRAIN DEATH

CLINICAL ASPECTS

Between full consciousness and complete unconsciousness, or coma, there lies a spectrum of severity. In complete coma, the patient cannot be aroused by any stimulus, however vigorous, or by any inner need (for example, hunger). Clearly, there are situations which are not as severe as coma, which now tend to be termed stupor, where the patient appears to be unresponsive, but can be aroused by vigorous or continuous external stimulation. Most neurologists use the terms 'obtunded' to suggest a patient who is not in stupor but whose mental faculties appear to be globally reduced, and where arousal is increasingly difficult.

The state of consciousness depends upon the normal function of the ascending reticular activating system (RAS), which lies within the brain stem from the lower third of the pons to the upper part of the mid brain (Figure 5.1). It has been shown that lesions beneath the RAS do not produce coma. For coma to be induced, both sides of the brain stem have to be involved.

Figure 5.1   **Position of the reticular activating system (RAS)**

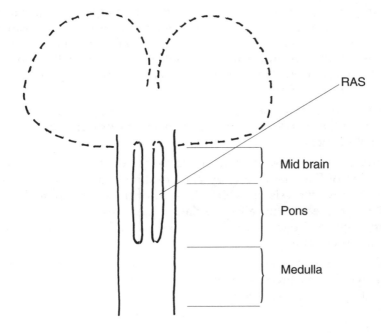

In coma, there is no sleep/wake cycle, and the eyes are closed. In patients who do not recover from coma, after two to three weeks, they merge into a persistent vegetative state, where there is a return of sleep/wake cycles and the eyes open and close appropriately with sleep, and normal respiration is maintained. These patients, however, show no evidence that they are responsive to any form of stimuli. The level of coma can be assessed using the Glasgow coma scale (see Chapter 3).

Given that stupor and coma require bilateral involvement of the RAS in the brain stem, the most common causes of stupor and coma are metabolic. In this group of disorders, some derangement of the body's internal metabolism has occurred, which suppresses the RAS, leading to stupor and coma. The importance of recognising metabolic abnormalities is that most are reversible. Patients are seen to slip via obtundation to stupor and coma. They may show evidence of tremor and involuntary short jerking movements (myoclonus), and seizure activity is not uncommon.

However, the commonest metabolic cause of coma is that associated with diabetes, where the patient's blood sugar may be either too high (hyperglycaemic coma) or too low (hypoglycaemic coma). A third form of coma in diabetes is associated with hyperosmolarity Prolonged hypoglycaemic coma has been associated with long term neurological deficit.

OSMOLAR COMA

The osmolarity of the blood relates to the relative proportions of anions and cations. The principle cation is sodium and, for practical purposes, osmolar coma relates to a low serum sodium (hyponatraemia). Stupor and coma supervene when the serum sodium concentration is below 120 mmol/l. However, it is more often a rapid fall in the serum sodium, rather than the absolute level, which is important.

Hyponatraemia may be seen with profuse vomiting and diarrhoea, in severe head injury, in association with carcinoma of the bronchus and in renal electrolyte disturbances.

The correction of the low sodium should be by water restriction. Overly rapid correction of hyponatraemia, by giving saline infusions, may lead to central pontine myelinolysis, in which the area of the central pons rapidly demyelinates. This leads clinically to a flaccid paralysis, some difficulty in swallowing, abnormal eye movements, profound imbalance (ataxia) and alterations in consciousness.

Thyroid disease may be associated with coma, particular in patients with an under active thyroid (myxoedema). Coma, in this situation, is classically associated with profound hypothermia.

Drug or alcohol intoxication is a major cause of coma, and is probably that most frequently seen in casualty departments.

Cerebrovascular accidents are another common cause of coma, usually when the lesion is major and produces distortion of the brain stem, which secondarily affects the RAS. Hence, a large infarct can cause swelling of a single hemisphere sufficient to produce distortion of the brain stem. Similarly, massive subarachnoid haemorrhage may have the same effect. Large intracerebral or intracerebellar haemorrhages may also have the same effect (see Chapter 7). Coma associated with head injury has been discussed in Chapter 3, and infections of the nervous system will been discussed in Chapter 11.

Although neurologists are frequently involved in the diagnosis of the cause of coma, given that the majority of cases are due to metabolic causes, the management is in the domain of physicians.

A patient presenting to a casualty department in coma requires immediate protection of the airway and, if necessary, assisted respiration. Appropriate investigations for metabolic causes (for example, blood sugar, serum sodium, etc) are carried out. Detailed neurological and clinical examination is required to identify the potential causes, supplemented by investigation such as an electroencephalogram and computerised tomography scanning, as appropriate. Provided a CT scan shows no mass lesion, a lumbar puncture may be indicated.

The prognosis of coma depends upon its cause but, in general, carries a serious prognosis. The best prognosis is seen with coma due to drug toxicity and the various metabolic causes (apart from anoxia – see below). A much poorer prognosis is seen in patients with structural lesions or head injury. In general terms, the length of coma is of poor prognostic significance, as is increasing age.

DIAGNOSIS OF BRAIN DEATH

To say that a patient is 'brain dead', implies that there has been functional death of the brain stem. When brain stem death occurs, there is no possible chance of recovery.

The problems surrounding brain death have become of considerable importance in recent years, mainly because of the increasing difficulty in deciding whether it is justifiable to maintain life indefinitely with artificial support in patients with very severe brain damage and, secondly, because of the difficult question of deciding whether a cerebral lesion is irreversible and death is imminent, so that viable organs for donation may be removed.

The United Kingdom criteria have been laid down by the Conference of Medical Royal Colleges and Faculties, and these state:

All of the following should co-exist:

1   the patient must be deeply comatosed. There should be no suspicion that this is due to central nervous system depressant drugs; primary hypothermia must have been excluded; and any metabolic or endocrine contribution to, or cause of, the coma must have been carefully assessed;

2   the patient must be being maintained on a ventilator because spontaneous respiration had previously become inadequate or had ceased altogether. Neuromuscular blocking agents must have been excluded as a cause of respiratory failure. Failure of neuromuscular transmission due to other causes may need to be excluded by use of a nerve stimulator;

3   there should be no doubt that the patient's condition is due to irremediable structural brain damage, and the diagnosis of the underlying cause of brain death should have been fully established.

Tests for brain death

There are fixed tests for confirming brain death, which indicate that all brain stem reflexes should be absent:

(a) the pupils are fixed in diameter and do not respond to sharp changes in the intensity of incident light;

(b) there is no corneal reflex;

(c) the vestibulo-ocular reflexes are absent. These are absent when no eye movement occurs during or after the slow injection of 20 mls of ice cold water into each external auditory meatus in turn, clear access to the tympanic membrane having been established by direct inspection. This test may be contraindicated on one side or another by local trauma;

(d) no motor response within the cranial nerve distribution can be elicited by adequate simulation of any somatic area;

(e) there is no gag reflex or reflex response to bronchial stimulation via suction catheter passed down the trachea; and

(f) no respiratory movement occurs when the patient is disconnected from a mechanical ventilator for long enough to ensure that the arterial carbon dioxide tension rises above the threshold for stimulating respiration, that is, a $PaCo_2$ must normally reach 6.7 kPa (50 mmHg). Hypoxia during disconnection should be prevented by delivering oxygen at 6 l/m through a catheter into the trachea.

In some countries, the above criteria are supplemented by the requirement of an isoelectric EEG. This is not necessary in the UK.

Given that spinal cord function can persist in the absence of brain stem function, the retention of the deep tendon reflexes does not preclude a diagnosis of brain stem death.

It is required that the tests should be repeated, in order to ensure that there is no observer error, by two independent clinicians. It is important that experienced clinicians, one of whom is a consultant, perform the tests. The timing of the interval between the tests is not fixed but, in most instances, it is 24 hours.

CHAPTER 6

EPILEPSY

DEFINITION

Although Jackson's (1873) definition of epilepsy derives from the latter half of the last century, it has stood the test of time. He defined epilepsy as being 'the name for occasional, sudden, excessive, rapid and local discharges of grey matter'.

Although the clinical manifestations of epileptic seizures differ, more recently, Chadwick, in 'Seizures, epilepsy and other episodic disorders in the brain', in *Disease of the Nervous System*, 10th edn, 1993, has defined an epileptic seizure as:

> ... an intermittent, stereotyped disturbance of consciousness, behaviour, emotion, motor function or sensation that, on clinical grounds, is believed to result from cortical neuronal discharge.

Thus, epilepsy can be defined as a condition in which seizures recur. In general terms, seizures can be divided into two groups, generalised and focal. Simplistically, generalised epilepsies arise from the deeper structures of the brain (Figure 6.1), whereas focal epilepsies arise from the cortex (Figure 6.2).

Figure 6.1   **Generalised epilepsy, the seizure discharge spreading to all parts of the cortex coequally**

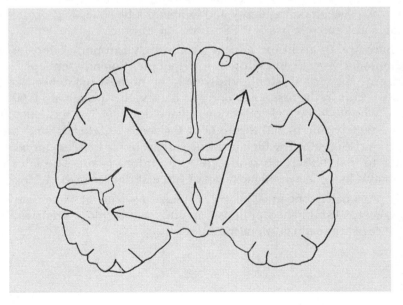

Figure 6.2   Focal epilepsy seizure, with discharge arising from one area of the cortex

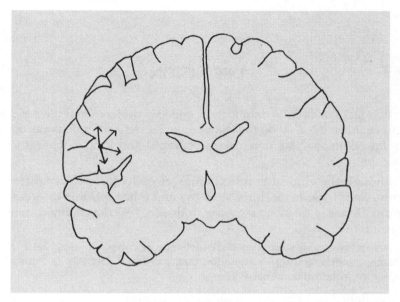

The generalised epilepsies comprise typical absence (formally known as *petit mal*), atypical absence, tonic clonic seizures (formally known as *grand mal*) and the myoclonic epilepsies, in particular, juvenile myoclonic epilepsy.

The focal epilepsies (otherwise known as partial epilepsies) arise from differing areas of the cortex, and are thus defined by the area from which they arise, for example, frontal lobe seizures, temporal lobe seizures (previously known as psychomotor epilepsy and temporal lobe epilepsy), seizures of the parietal lobes and seizures of the the occipital lobes.

There are, in addition, a large group of syndromic epilepsies which predominantly occur in children, for example, Rolandic epilepsy, West's Syndrome, Lennox Gastaut syndrome. The highest incidence of seizure activity occurs in the first few months of life and, by the age of 11, 50% of all people who will develop epilepsy will have done so. The incidence falls to approximately one in 200 throughout the teens to late 50s, and then the incidence rises again. The high incidence of risk in the first few months of life relates to metabolic factors affecting the infant brain. The later rise is attributable to the increased incidence of vascular disease in the ageing brain.

Approximately one in 60 people will have a seizure at some time in their life, whereas established epilepsy, having two or more seizures, has an incidence of approximately one in 200.

SYMPTOMATOLOGY OF SEIZURES

Primary generalised epilepsies

Absence seizures

This is predominantly a disease of childhood, and it rarely continues or develops beyond the age of 18. Children typically appear to 'switch off' for a few seconds, and may be observed to have flickering of the eyelids. Commonly, the attacks start around the early part of the child's educational life, and they are not infrequently first recognised by teachers rather than parents. A proportion of children with absence seizures will go on to develop generalised tonic clonic seizures.

Tonic clonic seizures

These are the most dramatic of all seizure types, because the seizure discharge arises from the deeper structures within the brain, and spreads out to all parts of the brain co-equally. There is immediate loss of consciousness, the individual having no warning whatsoever of the attack. The individual will usually become rigid in the first instance, and then go into the tonic clonic phase, where there is alternating relaxation and contraction of the musculature such that they appear to be shaking co-equally on both sides of the body (jactitation). If the tongue is between the teeth at the time of the onset of the fit then it may well be bitten, and there may be loss of sphincter tone, resulting in incontinence, predominantly of urine. These events are not specific to tonic clonic seizures, and are less frequently seen (in 10% to 15% of patients only) than are commonly imagined to occur.

The patient is at risk of self-harm during the initial part of the fit when they fall to the ground.

The majority of tonic clonic seizures are short lived, lasting two to three minutes at a time, and they occur at any time of the day. Following a seizure, the patient may be confused and restive, or may well sleep for several hours. If the patient goes on to have a second seizure without regaining full consciousness then the condition is diagnosed as status epilepticus.

It is important to recognise that consciousness is impaired at the onset of the seizure. A patient who describes bilateral jactitation, and claims to be aware of it, is, by definition, not suffering from a tonic clonic seizure.

Myoclonic epilepsy

In this condition, a patient typically has short lived 'jerks' which are symmetrical. They predominantly affect the arms or head, and may be associated with vocal utterances. These often occur in the situation of clear consciousness, and typically occur in the early morning. They may progress to generalised tonic clonic seizure activity.

One form of this type of epilepsy is inherited and is related to a gene disorder on chromosome 6.

The primary generalised epilepsies account for approximately 25% of all cases of adolescent/adult onset epilepsies.

Focal epilepsies

The phenomenology of focal epilepsies depends entirely upon the area of the cortex from which they arise. They can exist in two states, known as simple partial or complex partial seizures.

In simple partial seizures, awareness is retained throughout the event. Patients are aware that something is happening to them, whilst still being aware of their surroundings.

In complex partial seizures, awareness is lost and the patient is observed to be staring vacantly into space. They may have associated automatic movements (automatisms), which commonly consist of lip smacking or hand wringing. Volitional activity during an automatism is not possible, in that the automatisms themselves are primitive, stereotyped, repetitive movements, not driven by conscious demand.

Patients may progress from a simple partial seizure to a tonic clonic seizure (then known as a secondary generalisation: see Figure 6.3), or they may progress from a simple seizure to a complex seizure and then to a secondary generalisation. In the majority of instances, secondary generalisations occur nocturnally, whereas the partial seizure activity can occur throughout the day, with a predilection for the early morning and early evening. Not uncommonly, partial seizures are unrecognised, not only by the patient, but also by their medical attendants, and it is the development of a secondary generalisation which brings the patient to clinical attention.

Most partial seizures are of short duration (90 seconds to two minutes).

Frontal lobe seizures

In partial seizures arising from the frontal lobe, there is aversive head turning, away from the side of the electrical discharge.

Figure 6.3   Secondary generalisations: seizure discharge arises at the focal area of the cortex and then spreads to the deeper parts of the brain and triggers a secondary generalised seizure

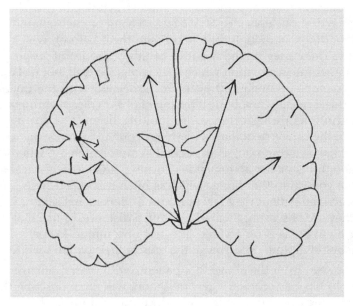

Frontoparietal seizures

In seizures arising from the motor strip, there is a characteristic 'march' of symptomatology, first described by Jackson, and hence known as the 'Jacksonian march'. Typically, the patient will develop focal jactitation, affecting one or other hand, then spreading up to the forearm, to the upper arm and to the face. These attacks are always unilateral. Focal sensory epilepsy arising from the sensory strip is much less common, but a similar march of sensory symptomatology occurs.

Following both of these focal seizures, there will be a period of paralysis in the motor form, or a continued sensory abnormality in the sensory form, known as Todd's paresis. This rarely lasts beyond 24 hours.

Occipital lobe seizures

In seizures arising from the occipital lobes, the patient usually describes visual symptoms including spots, flashes of light or patterns in one visual field. These forms of focal epilepsy are relatively uncommon, as is so called 'epileptic dizziness', when patients describe a feeling of giddiness, not associated with true rotational vertigo, which, when it occurs in the simple form, may be exceedingly difficult to differentiate from the vestibular dysfunction.

Temporal lobe seizures

By far the most common manifestation of partial seizures are those arising from the temporal lobes and their associated structures. In this situation, the patients often describe episodes of *déjà vu* (a feeling of intense familiarity with their surroundings as though they have been there before), which is always stereotyped. There may be the negative of this, episodes of *jamais vu*, where the patient goes into a situation which they recognise well, but feels strange to them. Perversions of smell and taste are associated with the uncus; visual hallucinations, typically involving a feeling of objects disappearing away from the individual, as though they were looking down the wrong end of a telescope, or the converse of that, with things coming towards them, changing size and shape, are common; as is visceral symptomatology, where a patient feels as though his or her abdomen is churning, arising as a warm sensation through the chest into the throat, which is often associated with a feeling of fear or panic. The patient may feel episodes of depersonalisation, where they may feel they are observing themselves from a distance, or feel that the world is passing them by as if on a video. It is not uncommon for patients to have more than one symptom occurring at the time of their partial seizure.

It can be seen from the above that patients with partial seizure activity, if they go on to have a secondary generalisation, will often describe the partial seizure occurring first thus giving rise to the term 'an aura' to the attack.

The partial epilepsies account for approximately 75% of adolescent/adult onset epilepsy.

CAUSES OF SEIZURES AND EPILEPSY

The majority of seizures, in epilepsy which develops in adult life, are regarded as idiopathic. Significant numbers of patients (up to 60%) will show no obvious causes for their seizure or epilepsy on routine investigations.

Seizures and epilepsy can be divided into acute symptomatic seizures, which occur acutely in response to a metabolic or cerebral insult, and remote symptomatic epilepsy, in which epilepsy develops in relation to a previous cerebral insult. These are not mutually exclusive, in that, for example, head injury can cause both acute symptomatic seizures and remote symptomatic epilepsy. It has been shown that, overall, the commonest causes of remote symptomatic epilepsy are vascular disease, accounting for 18% of cases, and tumour, accounting for 6%.

However, when age is taken into account, 49% of epilepsy arising in the elderly is due to underlying vascular disease. Tumours are rare below the age of 30, accounting for about 1%, but account for approximately 20% between the ages of 50 and 60. Trauma accounts for 3% of remote symptomatic epilepsy, and infection for 2%.

Acute symptomatic seizures

These seizures are usually associated with an encephalopathy, caused by either a disturbance in fluid or electrolyte balance, a metabolic disorder or drug induced. Acute seizure may be seen in drug withdrawal states, particularly from alcohol, barbiturates and benzodiazepines.

Remote symptomatic causes of epilepsy

Hypoxic/ischaemic cerebral insults, when the brain is starved of oxygen or blood (hypoxia and ischaemia respectively), carry a major risk of causing epilepsy. In the developing brain, remote symptomatic epilepsy is much less likely to develop, compared to a comparable insult in the adult brain, which is more likely to produce acute symptomatic seizures.

In patients who have complex partial seizures and who come to surgery (see below, p 104), the most common pathological reason is that of hippocampal sclerosis. The hippocampus is particularly sensitive to anoxia, and it has been suggested that prolonged or complicated febrile seizures in childhood may result in hippocampal sclerosis, and may be the etiological factor in some 20% of cases of adolescent or adult partial seizures.

Head injuries

The relationship between head injury and epilepsy has been extensively studied, both with respect to acute symptomatic seizures (those occurring within the first week of injury) and late post traumatic epilepsy.

It is clear that only specific types of head injury, that is, those which penetrate the dura or cause intracranial haematoma, carry a significant risk of post traumatic epilepsy, and, in general terms, the more severe the head injury, the higher the risk of post traumatic epilepsy.

Missile injuries

These have been studied in patients from various worldwide conflicts, from the First World War to the Vietnam War. In general, some 50% of patients with a missile injury will develop epilepsy. The risk is massively elevated in the first year after the injury, as compared to the general population (x 580), falling over the next 10 years but still remaining elevated (x 25).

Blunt head injuries

There have been two major studies on the effects of blunt head injury with respect to epilepsy. Jennett (*Epilepsy After Non Missile Head Injuries*, 2nd edition, 1975) studied a cohort of patients who had been admitted to a neurosurgical unit following head injuries. The other study, by Annegers *et al* ('Seizures after head trauma: a population study' (1980) 30 *Neurology* 638), used the record linkage system of the Mayo Clinic to identify a larger cohort (2,747 patients) with head injuries which had occurred between 1935 and 1974.

Jennett studied his cohort according to location and type of injury. Jennett's study shows that the severity of the injury, as judged by the presence of fracture, prolonged post traumatic amnesia, neurological deficit and intracranial haemorrhage, was associated with a higher incidence of early seizures. Twenty five per cent of patients with early seizures developed late epilepsy, compared to 3% of those without early seizures.

In the Annegers study, the minimal clinical criteria were an injury to the skull resulting in loss of consciousness, post traumatic amnesia or evidence of skull fracture. Annegers' team divided their patients into three groups, severe, moderate and mild. In the severe group, there was evidence of brain contusion, intracerebral or intracranial haematoma, or 24 hours of unconsciousness or amnesia. In the moderate group, there was the presence of a skull fracture, or 13–24 hours of unconsciousness or post traumatic amnesia, and in the mild group, there were shorter periods of unconsciousness or amnesia.

The risk of early seizures occurring within the first week after the injury was, for severe head injuries, 13.5% in children and 10.3% in adults. For late seizures the risk for patients with severe injuries was 7.1% at one year, and 11.5% at five years. For moderate injuries the figures were 0.7% and 1.6%, and for mild injuries, 0.1% and 0.6%. These latter figures, with respect to mild head injury, do not differ from normal population risk.

Both studies agree that the risk of developing late epilepsy as a consequence of a head injury requires that the injury is of sufficient severity to cause either dural tear (for example, via a depressed fracture) and/or the presence of intracerebral haematoma.

It has to be stressed that minor head injuries are not associated with any risk of developing late epilepsy.

The vast majority of late onset seizures occurring as a consequence of injury are focal seizures. However, it is often difficult to determine the phenomenology of partial seizures in the presence of associated brain injury.

The long term prognosis for patients with post traumatic epilepsy is not as good as for patients with a normal brain.

Post craniotomy seizures

The risk of developing epilepsy following a craniotomy depends on the reason for the craniotomy. About 20% of patients undergoing aneurysm surgery will develop seizures; the risk of arteriovenous malformations is around 50%, and that of spontaneous intracerebral haematoma is about 20%.

The risk following surgery for benign tumours is difficult to assess because of the progressive nature of the condition. About 20% of patients will develop seizures following surgery for meningioma, and about 15% of patients with frontal surgery for pituitary adenoma and craniopharyngioma.

Ventricular shunting procedures carry a 24% risk of seizure, while the risk of seizures following surgery for abscesses is exceptionally high, and virtually all patients will develop seizures with time.

Seven per cent of patients will have had their seizures within the first week following surgery and, of those who are going to develop seizures, 77% will develop them in the first year, and 92% within the first two years.

Intracranial tumours

Overall, about 30% of patients who have seizure activity associated with a tumour, will have their seizures as the first symptom. This figure reflects the difference according to tumour type, in that 80–90% of oligodendrogliomas are associated with epilepsy, 40–60% of meningiomas, 60–70% of astrocytomas and 30–40% of malignant gliomas. The risk of developing epilepsy either from a benign or a malignant glioma depends further on its location, being highest in patients with lesions in the frontoparietal or occipital lobes.

Given that a patient who presents with a focal seizure due to a tumour has a much greater probability that the tumour will be benign than malignant, this has lead to a considerable dilemma regarding the management of patients who have epilepsy as their only symptom of a tumour. Many neurologists would subscribe to the view that, provided the patient's epilepsy is well controlled and they have no other symptoms of disease in the nervous system, they would not recommend biopsy/resection/radiotherapy until there is evidence of associated symptomatology. This, however, is not the case with meningiomas, where surgery is usually undertaken.

Vascular disease

Overall, it has been estimated that cerebrovascular disease accounts for 15% of all patients with newly diagnosed epilepsy, the figure rising to 50% in the elderly. The figures are lowest for cerebral infarction (approximately 4%), compared with intracerebral haemorrhage (about 18%) and subarachnoid haemorrhage (28%). Seizures that come on following a cerebrovascular event usually occur within the first week, and are not highly predictive of late epilepsy.

INVESTIGATION OF PATIENTS WITH EPILEPSY

The diagnosis of epilepsy rests firmly on the clinical history, and all other investigations are ancillary, the diagnosis of epilepsy being clinical rather than laboratory based.

The most important investigation in a patient with epilepsy is a detailed neurological examination. Any abnormality found on that examination, particularly if it is asymmetrical, increases the likelihood of there being an intracranial cause for the epilepsy.

Skull X-rays were previously used routinely in the evaluation of a patient with epilepsy, but their use has, to a large extent, been superseded by CT/MR techniques. However, the skull X-ray remains useful in identifying any possible skull fracture and to show evidence of long standing raised intracranial pressure (erosion of the posterior clinoids). CT/MR scanning has become routine in the investigation of patients with seizure disorder. Although MR scanning is not as freely available, it is the investigation of choice, since the detail of the intracranial contents is far superior to that shown by CT. Of particular importance is the fact that sequence of MR scanning have been developed which permit the identification of hippocampal sclerosis, which is the major aetiological factor in the majority of patients with adolescent or adult onset epilepsy. However, if MR scanning is not available, then all patients with epilepsy ought to have a CT scan, irrespective of whether their clinical examination is normal or not.

The use of the electroencephalogram (EEG) is surrounded by much mystique. There appears to be a belief that an EEG will diagnose epilepsy. This is only the case if the patient has a seizure during the electrical recording. In general terms, 70% of all *inter* ictal (that is, between seizures) EEGs will be normal.

In the primary generalised epilepsies, there is much more likelihood of identifying an abnormal seizure discharge (commonly, spike, poly spike and wave) than in the partial epilepsies. In many patients with a partial epilepsy, the only abnormality on a routine EEG may be an excess of slow activity (theta to delta), without convincing evidence of epileptic discharges. The possibility of identifying an epileptic discharge is increased by activation procedures (hyperventilation/photic stimulation).

Increasingly, 24 hour recording of the EEG has been undertaken, recognising that the routine EEG, which lasts about 30 minutes, is a small snapshot in time. The 24 hour record requires admission to hospital in the majority of instances, as the technology is insufficiently robust to permit the patient to be tested as an out patient. The information gained, however, from 24 hour records considerably increases the likelihood of identifying a seizure discharge compared to a routine half hour record.

Highly specialist centres combine 24 hour recording with simultaneous video recording of the patient, so that the patient's behaviour can be identified and correlated with the electrical activity seen by the EEG. This, however, is not a routine investigation.

DIFFERENTIAL DIAGNOSIS OF EPILEPSY

The most common misdiagnosis of epilepsy is that of syncope (faint). Almost all individuals have been aware of an episode of syncope at some time in their life.

In syncope, there is impaired oxygen supply to the brain, usually as a consequence of impaired blood flow. The onset is generally gradual and, if the event occurs when the individual is standing, in most instances they will slowly subside to the ground, rather than fall rigidly as is commonly seen in seizures.

Once the blood supply to the brain has been re-established, then the individual is rapidly back into clear consciousness, in contradistinction to patients with seizure activity, where confusion is ubiquitous. However, in a major episode of syncope the patient can be observed to have focal twitching movements which do not amount to the jactitation occurring in patients with a true tonic clonic seizure. Such events often lead to an erroneous diagnosis of epilepsy, and underline the importance of obtaining a detailed history of the event before making a diagnosis of epilepsy.

Transient episodes of brain ischaemia, either due to transient ischaemic attacks (see Chapter 7) or migraine, may occasionally produce symptoms which are difficult to distinguish from seizures. This is particularly true in migraine, where unconsciousness may occur, although this is usually of a syncopal type.

Some migraine events may progress into a frank epileptic seizure; in other instances, the cause of the migraine may also be a cause of seizure activity, particularly in the case of arteriovenous malformations (see Chapter 7).

TREATMENT OF EPILEPSY

Patients suffering from epilepsy, and, indeed, society in general, continue to have major misconceptions and fears regarding the disease. It is important, therefore, that the institution of drug therapy is also accompanied by a detailed explanation of the reasons for therapy, the limitations the disease will place upon the individual, and also to dispel the many myths which surround the condition.

A common method of explaining the causes of seizure activity to an individual suffering from the disease is to employ the so called threshold model (Figure 6.4). This relies on the fact that any given nerve cell has a resting threshold level. A stimulus which exceeds the normal threshold will allow the cell to fire in a programmed manner leading to a recognisable result. However, if the threshold level is lowered, then the same stimulus will set the cell off to fire at a lower level, and may well produce a bizarre result, for example, a seizure.

On the basis of this model, it is useful to suggest to patients that the institution of drug therapy will simply elevate their lowered threshold level to somewhere within the normal range and, hence, their seizures will be suppressed by the drug therapy. Using this model, it is possible to educate patients to avoid those situations which may well depress the threshold level (sleep deprivation, food deprivation and alcohol).

Figure 6.4   Threshold model of epilepsy. Nerve cells have a resting membrane potential of minus 70 microvolts and a stimulus of greater than that is required to trigger the cell to fire. If the cell is triggered at a lower level, a bizarre result, that is, a seizure, occurs.

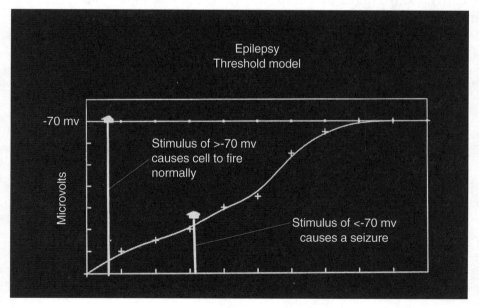

(a) The threshold has not achieved adult levels as quickly as expected.

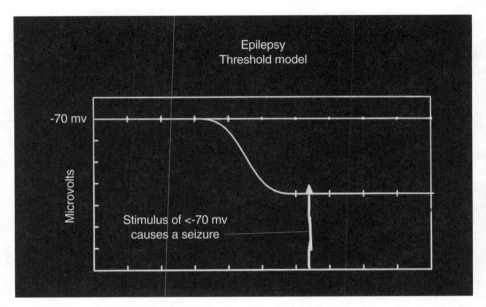

(b) The threshold has been permanently reduced

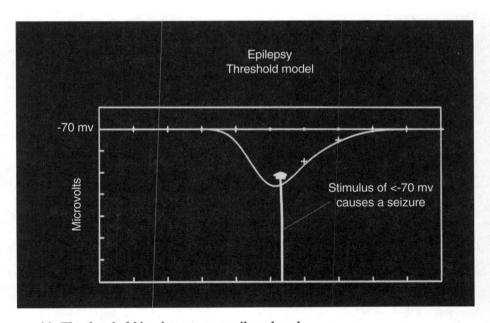

(c) The threshold has been temporarily reduced

For adolescents and adults, the question uppermost in their mind is that relating to driving. The current regulations are that, after a single seizure or recurrent seizures, the individual must stop driving until they have been one year free of seizures, whether or not they are taking medication. The only exceptions to this rule are if the seizure has been deemed to be 'evoked', that is, there has been a particular cause for the seizure which has been identified, and that cause is not going to be repeated. The commonest situation where this pertains is in relation to adverse reactions to drugs.

Employment is also a major consideration. It would be unwise for patients with frequent seizures to work at heights or close to water. The history of seizure activity precludes certain occupations (airline pilot, taxi driver, train driver, etc). There remains, however, a very considerable belief in patients with epilepsy that they are discriminated against in employment because of their disease process.

Females need to be advised of the risks during pregnancy, both from the disease itself, and from any concomitant medication.

These comments suggest, therefore, that the management of a patient with epilepsy should only be undertaken by someone who has sufficient expertise to be able to deal with the points raised above, in addition to being able to deal with other forms of therapy.

Drug therapy

If a patient presents with a series of seizures over a short interval of time, there is usually no difficulty in establishing the need for anticonvulsant medication. Difficulties arise from a single seizure and in patients who have long gaps between their seizures. Most neurologists would withhold drug therapy after a single seizure, unless there is evidence of a clear cut abnormality on an EEG or there is evidence of a progressive disorder of brain which is known to provoke seizure activity. This is based on the fact that one in 60 of the population will have seizure at some time during their life, but only one in 200 go on to have a second seizure and, thus, established epilepsy.

When dealing with established epilepsy, the difficulty is in deciding what constitutes the short interval of time, as mentioned above. If seizures are widely separated, then the risk of side effects on anticonvulsants may outweigh the benefit from their introduction. In routine practice, seizures occurring less than 12 months apart would be an indication for instituting anticonvulsant drug therapy.

All anticonvulsant drugs have side effects and their side effect profile is increased when two anticonvulsants are taken together. They are exponentially increased when a third, fourth or fifth anticonvulsant is added. For this reason, patients should be started on a single anticonvulsant drug (monotherapy) and, with such a regime, some 70–80% of patients can be expected to enter a long remission (greater than two years). Polypharmacy should therefore be reserved for the group of patients whose seizures are not brought under control by a single anticonvulsant.

It may be evident from the initial investigation of the patient that their seizures are unlikely to come under good control because of the presence of structural disease or the presence of a progressive neurological disorder. In patients whose initial evaluation failed to reveal such abnormalities, the failure of monotherapy is the indication for re-investigation to ensure that a potentially treatable intracerebral disorder has not developed in the interim.

The choice of drug to be used in monotherapy depends on knowledge of comparative efficacy and toxicity. The common anticonvulsants presently used are listed in Table 6.1.

Table 6.1   Commonly used anticonvulsants

Generic name	Proprietary name
Sodium valproate	Epilim
Carbamazepine	Tegretol
Phenytoin	Epanutin
Lamotrigine	Lamictal
Gabapentin	Neurontin
Vigabatrin	Sabril
Clonazepam	Rivotril
Topiramate	Topamax
Ethosuximide	Zarontin
Primidone	Mysoline
Phenobarbitone	Phenobarbitone

Toxic reactions can be classified as acute dose related, acute idiosyncratic, chronic and teratogenicity. Acute dose related toxicity is usually associated with sedation and nystagmus, and, as the blood levels increase, ataxia, dysarthria and ultimately confusion and drowsiness. This can be remedied by reducing the dose. Idiosyncratic toxicity is seen particularly with phenytoin, carbamazepine and lamotrigine, which may cause a rash (in up to 18% of patients treated with carbamazepine).

Chronic toxicity

The most important effect of chronic toxicity, from the patient's point of view, is impairment of higher intellectual function, impairment of both memory and concentration and general slowing of mentation.

Teratogenicity

All anticonvulsant drugs have a risk of causing foetal malformations, and that risk must be discussed in detail with female patients suffering from epilepsy.

Surgical treatment

It is becoming increasing common to refer patients with uncontrolled epilepsy for consideration of surgical removal of that part of the brain which causes their seizures. There are now well defined parameters which have to be satisfied before a patient is deemed amenable to surgery and, with patients who fulfil all the criteria, then the risk of such surgery is low, and the probability of seizure improvement or cessation is high. This, however, is a technique for specialist centres.

DEATH AS A CONSEQUENCE OF EPILEPSY

The mortality ratio for patients with epilepsy is some two to three times higher than an age matched population. This is in part due to the aetiology of epilepsy in some patients (tumours, etc). There is, however, the risk of trauma during a seizure (head trauma, suffocation, drowning).

Recently recognised is the fact that patients who do have uncontrolled epilepsy are at risk of sudden unexplained death, that is, despite careful investigation and post mortem, no identifiable cause for the death can be found. This syndrome now goes by the title 'sudden unexpected death in epilepsy' (SUDEP). This syndrome is encompassed by certain parameters, which are:

(a) that the patient has to suffer from epilepsy;

(b) that the patient has died unexpectedly while in a reasonable state of health;

(c) that the death occurred suddenly (in minutes) when known;

(d) that the death occurred during normal activities and benign circumstances; and

(e) that no obvious medical cause of death was found, and the death was not the direct cause of the seizure or status epilepticus.

The main risk factor for SUDEP appears to be seizure severity. The risk appears to be higher for acquired epilepsy, particularly that following traumatic brain injury or encephalitis, than for idiopathic epilepsy, where the potential risk factors include the male sex, younger age of onset and partial onset seizures. The risks of SUDEP vary, depending on which series has been published, from one in 100 to one in 1,000 per year. It is believed that many of these deaths may be associated with cardiac dysrhythmias.

A patient with epilepsy presents a particular challenge in terms of diagnosis and management, and it is regrettable that not all patients who suffer from epilepsy are under the care of neurologists who understand the condition.

CHAPTER 7

VASCULAR DISEASE

INTRODUCTION

The brain derives its blood supply from the two internal carotid arteries, which supply roughly the anterior two thirds of the brain, and from the two vertebral arteries, which supply the posterior third of the brain (Figure 7.1).

Figure 7.1   Blood supply to the brain

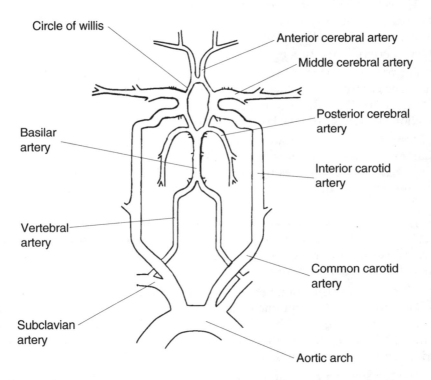

The internal carotid artery divides into two major branches, the anterior cerebral artery and the middle cerebral artery. The anterior cerebral artery supplies the anterior and medial parts of the cerebral hemisphere. The middle cerebral artery divides into anywhere from two to four branches which supply the lateral parts of the cerebral hemisphere.

The vertebral arteries join within the skull to form the basilar artery, and thus the vertebrobasilar system supplies the structures of the posterior fossa. The basilar artery continues and divides into the posterior cerebral arteries, which supply the occipital lobes. There is anastamosis between these vessels at the Circle of Willis. The posterior cerebral artery communicates with the internal carotid via the posterior communicating artery, and the anterior cerebral arteries combine via the anterior communicating artery. The arteries within the brain are end arteries, that is, they supply a given territory, but do not anastomose or branch with other arterial systems.

The venous drains from the brain are via the superior sagittal sinus, the inferior sagittal sinus and the straight sinus into the jugular vein. In contradistinction to the arterial supply, there are rich anastomoses between the venous systems in the brain and the meninges, skull, scalp and nasal sinuses.

The cerebral blood flow remains at a constant level between mean arterial pressures of 60–100 mm Hg. This is known as auto regulation. As a consequence of this, the brain can maintain its blood supply through a wide range of arterial pressure.

For practical purposes, vascular disease affecting the brain can be divided into transient ischaemic attacks (TIAs), and stroke or cerebrovascular accident (CVA). In the TIA, there is an acute loss of cerebral function or monocular function (amaurosis fugax), lasting less than 24 hours.

A stroke consists of rapidly developing clinical symptoms and/or signs of focal, or at times global, loss of cerebral function, the symptoms lasting more than 24 hours or progressing to death. A global loss of cerebral function applies to patients in deep coma and to those with sub arachnoid haemorrhage.

There is clearly a wide range of severity, from a CVA with recovery occurring in a few days, through to persistent disability to death. It has been variously estimated that between 15% and 25% of patients who have their first stroke have a past history of TIAs.

Although the distinction between a TIA and a stroke is arbitrary, based on 24 hour duration of symptomatology, it is of importance, in that, since short lived symptomatology, as in a TIA, permits detailed investigation of the cause of the TIA, this should lead to corrective measures, which may prevent a more serious stroke occurring with time.

The concept of a reversal of ischaemic neurological deficit (RIND) has also been suggested. These are patients who have symptoms of an acute ischaemic stroke, which last for between 48 and 72 hours, and then resolve, leaving the patient without neurological deficit. It is generally accepted that these patients should be investigated as for a TIA.

TRANSIENT ISCHAEMIC ATTACK (TIA)

TIAs can occur in either the carotid or in the vertebrobasilar distribution. Fifty per cent of patients will describe abrupt onset of weakness or clumsiness, often associated with a feeling of heaviness in the upper limb, the lower limb or the face, or in various combinations occurring on one side of the body. Sensory symptoms of numbness, tingling or deadness occur in some 35% of patients. In carotid TIAs, speech may be dysphasic. In vertebrobasilar TIAs, speech may be dysarthric.

Symptoms occurring simultaneously and bilaterally usually indicate vertebrobasilar TIA. Such symptoms as vertigo, diplopia, dysphagia, unsteadiness, tinnitus, drop attacks and dysarthria occurring in combination are suggestive of vertebrobasilar TIAs. However, any of the symptoms occurring alone could be the result of a more global brain involvement. Patients with TIAs, whether they are vertebrobasilar or carotid, do not lose consciousness.

Patients who develop loss of vision in one eye (amaurosis fugax) normally feel as though a blind has descended over one half of the visual field in the horizontal plane, and often describe the onset or resolution as being like a blind coming up or down. In the majority of instances, the symptoms wear off within an hour.

About 80% of TIAs are in the carotid territory and about 20% are in the vertebrobasilar territory.

In the situation of a TIA, the brain is the 'end organ'. Whatever abnormality is causing the TIA, it has to lie outside the brain itself. It is convenient to think of abnormalities which cause TIAs as being due to either failure in the pump (the heart), the pipes (the blood vessels), or the fluid itself (the blood).

With respect to the heart, the abnormalities include disorders of rhythm, disorders of the valves and disorder of the heart muscle itself. With respect to the blood vessels, the commonest abnormality is atheroma. With respect to the blood, anything which causes the blood to thicken (excess white cells, excess red cells, excess platelets) can cause TIAs.

The investigation of a patient with TIA, therefore, involves a clinical examination, primarily to ensure that there is no evidence of residual neurological deficit, and also in particular to listen over the carotid arteries for the presence of bruits which would indicate the possibility of carotid stenosis.

Investigation is undertaken to identify the source of emboli. It is important that a brain scan is carried out, in order to exclude those occasional patients who otherwise give a typical history of TIA, who have an underlying structural abnormality (tumour, subdural haematoma).

Disorders of the heart are assessed by chest X-ray, electrocardiogram (ECG), auscultation and, increasingly, echocardiography. Diseases of the blood vessels are assessed by ultrasound of the carotid arteries which, if suggestive of significant stenosis, is then followed by angiography. Diseases of the blood are assessed by haematological investigations, such as full blood count and erythrocyte sedimentation rate (ESR).

If these routine investigations fail to identify an appropriate cause for the TIA, then more detailed investigations, particularly in the younger person, looking for evidence of antiphosphalipid syndrome or systemic lupus erythematosus, are appropriate.

The management of a patient with TIA is commonly antiplatelet therapy with, at present, a low dose (75 mgs) of aspirin.

CEREBRAL INFARCTION

In the majority of patients with a stroke, there is a clear history of the sudden onset of neurological deficit, or the patient wakens in the morning aware that something is different from the night before. The deficit usually becomes stable between 12 and 24 hours later and, if the patient survives, recovery commences within a few days. The severity, however, can range, as noted previously, from a trivial deficit, which has cleared within 48 hours, to a persistent deficit to death.

Such a presentation is virtually symbolic of stroke, whether due to infarction or cerebral haemorrhage, but there remains a 5% chance of an alternate underlying cause, for example, a subdural haematoma, tumour or abscess. Therefore, in differentiating between cerebral haemorrhage and infarction, a CT scan should be undertaken in all stroke patients to exclude the rare causes.

In the anterior circulation, occlusion of the internal carotid or a haematoma in the cerebral hemisphere causes a sudden onset of contralateral hemiparesis affecting the face and the upper and lower limbs. There may be a corresponding sensory deficit. Since the horizontal pathways of the second optic nerve are involved, there would be homonymous hemianopia. If the left (dominant) hemisphere is involved, there will be dysphasia. If the right hemisphere is involved, there will be evidence of neglect on the visuospatial abnormalities.

If the haemorrhage is sufficiently large to cause herniation, then coma occurs, usually within 24 hours, in contradistinction to large ischaemic infarcts, where coma supervenes after two to three days as cerebral oedema develops. Such total anterior circulation infarcts account for about 15% of all strokes.

Partial anterior circulation syndromes account for about 35% of strokes. In this case, the infarct causes a more restricted clinical syndrome, haematomata occurring in the frontal or temporal lobe. The motor weakness usually affects only two components, either face and arm, face and leg or arm and leg, and the disturbance of higher cortical function is more restricted. Such lesions usually arise from occlusion of the middle cerebral artery. If the anterior cerebral artery is involved there is contralateral weakness of the lower limb.

Lacunar syndromes are due to small infarcts which are sometimes visualised on CT scanning, but are readily visualised by MR scanning. These lesions occur in the deep white matter, rather than in the cortex, and therefore there is no impairment of the visual field, and there is no disturbance of higher intellectual function. If the infarct is in the internal capsule, this can produce a pure motor stroke (50%) or a sensory motor stroke (25%). A pure sensory stroke is rarer (5%). Lacunar strokes account for about 25% of all strokes. Intracerebral haemorrhage is rarely seen in this situation.

In the posterior circulation, infarcts account for about 25% of all strokes occurring in the brain stem, the cerebellum or in the occipital lobes. The prognosis for posterior circulation strokes is, in general, much better than for anterior circulation strokes, mortality being very low. The exception to this is in patients with primary cerebellar haematomata, or strokes where there may be sudden deterioration in consciousness occurring within the first 48 hours after the onset of a stroke. It is thought that the swelling associated with either the haematoma or the oedema from the infarct causes obstruction of the aqueduct leading to hydrocephalus. If this is rapidly removed surgically, then the patient may well make a reasonable recovery. In the absence of surgery, however, the prognosis is very poor.

BOUNDARY ZONE (WATERSHED) INFARCTS

Because the arteries that supply the brain are 'end arteries', there are boundaries between the circulations, the watershed zones. The boundary between the supply of the anterior cerebral artery and the middle cerebral artery occurs in the frontal parasagittal area; between the middle cerebral artery and the posterior cerebral artery, the boundary occurs in the parietal and occipital areas.

Watershed infarcts typically occur in situations of sustained hypotension, such as following cardiac arrest or any other cause of sustained hypotension. All patients presenting with stroke ought to have a CT scan carried out in the first few hours after the stroke; this may well be negative, but has at least excluded an intracerebral haemorrhage. If this stroke is relatively mild, then further investigation, as for a TIA, should be undertaken in the acute phase.

The management of patients with stroke, from whatever cause, has been the subject of a consensus statement from The Royal Colleges (1988). This notes:

(a) make a correct diagnosis of stroke verses not stroke;

(b) establish the reason for the stroke in terms of its pathological type (infarct or haemorrhage) and underlying cause, particularly if treatable (atherothromboembolism, cardiogenic embolism, vascular malformation); and

(c) unless the patient is very elderly, seriously handicapped or is expected to die, rapidly attempt to reduce early mortality and later disability by:

- maintenance of pulmonary, cardiovascular, fluid, electrolyte and nutritional homeostasis;

- avoidance, recognition and treatment of systemic complications;

- avoidance, recognition and treatment of early cause of neurological deterioration;

- minimise the extent of irreversible cerebral infarction;

- rehabilitate patients surviving the first few days;

- initiate secondary prevention in patients who have had benefit; and

- treat any coincidental disorders such a cardiac failure, angina, claudication and aortic aneurysm.

It is obvious from the above that this is an active management of the patient with stroke.

Some 3% of patients presenting with an acute stroke will develop seizure activity, which should be treated symptomatically.

The question of whether or not to lower blood pressure in the acute phase of stroke is more difficult. The stroke itself can cause a degree of hypertension, which will settle spontaneously with time. In general, levels of hypertension which would induce antihypertensive treatment if seen for the first time should probably be treated. Hypotension is best treated by removing the cause.

With respect to cerebral infarction, there are no routine treatments which, if given early, will improve the outlook for a patient with stroke, although many different drugs and combinations have been tried.

With primary cerebral haemorrhage, the same management applies as to an ischaemic stroke. There is no consensus as to whether or not haematomata ought to be evacuated when identified, or only if the patient shows evidence of deterioration.

Given that most intracerebral haematomata shrink with the passage of time, it would seem more sensible to monitor the patient closely, and only to intervene to remove the haematoma should there be any deterioration.

SUBARACHNOID HAEMORRHAGE

Subarachnoid haemorrhage (SAH), as the name implies, is the extravasation of blood into the subarachnoid space. In 75% of cases, this is due to a ruptured saccular aneurysm. In 5–10% of cases, it is due to bleeding from arterial venous malformation. There remains a further 10–20% of patients, in whom no obvious cause is found, the rarer causes (bleeding disorders, infections, cerebral arteriopathies, eclampsia) having been excluded.

Characteristically, the symptoms appear abruptly; however, about 10% of patients describe a gradual onset. The predominant symptoms are headache, vomiting and disturbance of consciousness, the latter being either transient or prolonged. With respect to the headache, many patients say that they feel as though they have been kicked in the head or that they have experienced a headache, the like of which they have never experienced before. Occasionally, the patient will say that the headache follows something going 'pop' within their head.

Between 40% and 60% of patients will have had prior warning symptoms over the preceding few weeks. These usually consist of mild attacks of head, face or neck pain lasting less than a few hours. Occasionally, more specific symptoms, such as diplopia and visual obscurations, may precede the definitive SAH.

About 50% of patients will experience vomiting at the onset. Some 50% of patients will have an episode of loss of consciousness, usually associated with an initial headache. However, 10% arrive in hospital in a coma and a further 10% are confused. Some 20% of patients will develop seizure activity at the onset of the bleeding.

About a third of patients with SAH appear to have a precipitating event. The commonest events were lifting or bending (12%), defecation (5%), sexual intercourse (4%), emotional upsets (4%), a head injury (3%) and coughing (2%).

The clinical examination of a patient with SAH will reveal neck stiffness and there may be retinal or subhyloid haemorrhages. The history of SAH in its full manifestation is so typical as not to be missed. The patients will always stress that they have never had a headache like this previously; even patients who have been long standing migrainers are always able to differentiate the headache of SAH from that of their migraine.

SAH figures high in the differential diagnosis of the patient admitted in coma.

Investigation and treatment

The vast majority of patients with SAH have a bleed from a saccular aneurysm. This develops at the bifurcation of arteries, and the thin walled aneurysm slowly increases in size. Contained within the aneurysm there may be a clot. Multiple aneurysms are not uncommon, and there is a familial incidence.

Investigation is with CT scanning which, in the first 24 hours, will show blood within the intracranial cavity in over 90% of cases. A negative scan, therefore, does not exclude diagnosis of an SAH in a patient with an otherwise typical history, in which case lumbar puncture is indicated. Once an SAH has been identified, then its cause should be identified with angiography.

Of those patients with subarachnoid haemorrhages who die, half will do so in the first month, and half of those will die on the first day. Patients who present in coma and elderly patients fare worse than younger patients.

If an aneurysm has been demonstrated, there is a 10% risk of re-bleeding within the first 24 hours, and a risk of about 30% of doing so during the first few weeks. Management is by 'clipping' the aneurysm which carries its own risks. About 50% of patients who survive subarachnoid haemorrhage are left with permanent deficits in terms of cerebral function. Some 20% of patients with SAH will develop hydrocephalus. The majority do so in the early phase of the illness, but this can be a late complication, and late deterioration in a patient with SAH should prompt further investigation to identify if hydrocephalus is present.

Hyponatremia (low serum sodium: see Chapter 5) will develop in about a third of patients usually in the first or second week after the SAH.

INTRACRANIAL VENOUS THROMBOSIS

Thrombosis of the dural sinus may produce a relatively restricted picture similar to benign intracranial hypertension (see Chapter 10). Infarction of the cerebral veins, however, is much more likely to cause venous infarctions.

Local conditions which cause intracranial venous thrombosis are head injury, intracranial surgery, nasopharyngeal sepsis and catheterisation of the jugular vein. Numerous systemic disorders can likewise cause the same syndrome, particularly dehydration, septicaemia, pregnancy and oral contraceptives.

In venous infarction, the patients tend to present with an encephalopathy, coming on over days or weeks, with headache, partial and generalised seizure, confusion, decline in conscious levels and sometimes focal neurological deficits such as hemiparesis.

The diagnosis of cerebral vein thrombosis is more often achieved by exclusion of other causes than by direct diagnosis.

HYPERTENSIVE ENCEPHALOPATHY

The clinical picture is of increasingly severe headache over several days, associated with nausea, vomiting and mental slowing. This progresses to frank confusion, blurring of vision, focal and generalised seizures, declining levels of consciousness and papilledema. These features are seen with an acute rise in blood pressure which is sufficiently high to breach cerebral autoregulation and is, therefore, seen particularly in eclampsia and stimulant drug overdose.

TEMPORAL ARTERITIS

This is a condition of later life, most commonly occurring after the age of 55. It may occur in isolation or in association with polymyalgia rheumatica (see Chapter 13). In patients with temporal arteritis, there is pain over the temple which often spreads to the side of the head. The pain is described as superficial, being 'on the head' rather than 'in the head'. Patients are often aware that the temporal arteries themselves are exquisitely tender to touch. Given that the condition affects not only the temporal artery, but most of the cranial arteries, there is often associated jaw claudication, in that, if a patient chews or talks for a long time, they develop pain and aching in the jaw muscles which is relieved by rest. There can be visual disturbance, from obscuration through to complete loss of vision, and transient ischaemic attacks, when strokes can occur. Often the patients feel a general systemic upset with non specific malaise and fever.

The condition is currently treatable by steroids, which are given in high doses in the initial phases, and are slowly tapered over a period of 12–18 months. Recurrence after that time is unusual.

There has been considerable debate as to whether temporal artery biopsy is indicated to actually demonstrate the inflammation of the artery wall or whether reliance can be placed on the elevated ESR. The latter is raised in about 98% of all patients with temporal arteritis, although there are occasional patients who have the full blown disorder with an entirely normal ESR.

The advantages of doing a temporal artery biopsy have to be set against the risks of the condition, the most important of which are necrosis of the skin over the front of the forehead, and the fact that it takes time to set up the necessary surgical team. During that time, further complications from the arteritis may arise. The majority of neurologists would, therefore, simply obtain blood for an ESR and treat the patient for 48 hours with steroids. If there has been no response after 48 hours, then the condition is unlikely to be temporal arteritis. If there has been a dramatic response, then the diagnosis is proven. A repeat ESR will then show a fall if it has been elevated. The rationale for this approach is that the potential risk of 48 hours of steroids is far less than the potential risk of temporal artery biopsy. Once established on treatment, the patient can be monitored according to their ESR, and their drug dose adjusted accordingly. The patients have to be made aware of the potential side effects of steroids.

CHAPTER 8

DEMYELINATING DISORDERS

INTRODUCTION

The demyelinating disorders encompass a wide range of conditions where the primary pathological event is a loss of myelin within the central nervous system. The majority of these are mediated by abnormalities in the immune system.

Multiple sclerosis (MS) affects the myelin sheaths, which constitute the white matter within the brain. Therefore, the presentation of a young patient with damage to white matter tracts within the central nervous system, particularly if affecting the optic nerve, brain stem and spinal cord, would lead to a high clinical suspicion of MS. However, there is no single presentation which is diagnostic of MS in its own right; rather, when there is evidence of damage to the nervous system at more than one site (dissemination in place) and at different times (dissemination in time), then the situation is characteristic of a patient with MS.

Therefore, symptoms of white matter involvement, due to demyelination, can occur as isolated events although, when these patients are followed over a protracted period of time, clinical evidence of multiple sclerosis often becomes much more apparent.

OPTIC NEURITIS (RETROBULBAR NEURITIS)

Optic neuritis typically presents with painful eye movements, rapidly followed by, or accompanied by from the onset, distortion and blurring of vision. Some patients are initially aware of loss of colour vision. Typically, the visual loss is in the centre of the visual field (scotoma: see Figure 8.1), and the patient is therefore aware of a loss of central vision with preservation of vision around the periphery. The degree of visual loss can be anything from mild blurring through to complete blindness.

The symptoms develop fully over a period of 72 to 96 hours; the pain then commonly subsides and there is improvement in vision, with the majority (90%) of patients considering themselves to be normal within three to four months.

The diagnosis of optic neuritis is always by exclusion, in that compressive lesions of the optic nerve, deriving either from invasion from the subjacent sinuses, tumours within the orbit, or tumours within the nerve itself, must be

Figure 8.1 **Visual field, showing area in which central scotoma causes loss of vision**

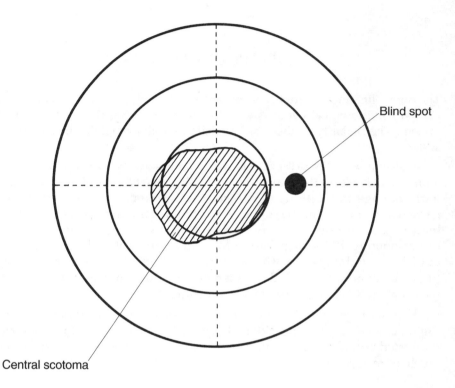

Blind spot

Central scotoma

excluded. In the older patient, anterior ischaemic optic neuropathy, due to vascular disease, may be a diagnostic trap. There is also an inherited form of optic atrophy (Leber's disease) which, because of a maternal mitochondrial inheritance, is expressed only in the male. The presentation of Leber's disease, although commonly that of slowly evolving visual loss, can be confused with that of an acute optic neuritis.

The exclusion of compressive lesions required when investigating optic neuritis is best carried out by magnetic resonance scanning of the eye and orbit. Computerised tomography scanning may be more helpful with patients that are likely to have sinus infection. The visual evoked response will show delay and abnormalities of the wave form in the majority of patients.

The treatment of optic neuritis is determined by its aetiology. In the case of isolated disease, there remains considerable debate as to whether or not the early institution of steroids (methylprednisolone) alters the subsequent course of the disease. Some argue that the prospect for good recovery of vision is enhanced by using intravenous steroids, whereas others feel that steroids should only be given if the unaffected eye is already compromised by concurrent ocular disease or previous optic neuritis.

Bilateral simultaneous optic neuritis does occur. It is more common in children, where it has a very benign prognosis, full recovery being the expected outcome. It is less common in the adult, and has a less predictable outcome. There is, however, a very low risk of the subsequent development of MS.

Given that some 50% of patients with MS will have involvement of the optic nerve at some time during their disease, there is considerable anxiety over the risk of developing MS after an isolated episode of optic neuritis. The risk is increased if there is a recurrence of optic neuritis, either in the same or the other eye, or if there is sequential optic neuritis. However, the major factor in determining risk is the duration of follow up from the original event. The highest risk period appears to be the first five years, with some 35% of patients going on to develop generalised multiple sclerosis during that period of time. However, the longer the follow up, the more patients will be shown to have generalised disease, and figures vary between 38% and 78% of patients over the long term.

TRANSVERSE MYELITIS

In this condition, there is involvement of the descending motor pathways and ascending sensory pathways within the spinal cord, usually associated with bladder dysfunction. As a consequence of the motor involvement, there is ascending weakness from the feet upwards to the trunk, usually evolving over a period of one to three days. The degree of weakness is usually profound, the patient being unable to walk.

Sensory disturbance is coincident in time with the motor disturbance, the numbness gradually ascending from the feet to a variable position on the trunk, indicating involvement at some level of the dorsal spinal cord. Occasionally, one or other arm may be involved.

Investigation of transverse myelitis is with imaging of the spine, preferably MR, or with CT myelography, to exclude compressive lesions and inflammatory disorders. With respect to treatment (usually with intravenous steroid), the same reservations apply as to the treatment of optic neuritis. There is, however, a general assumption that the earlier steroid therapy is instituted, the more favourable the outcome. Recovery is usually slow, over a period of weeks to months, and may well be incomplete. It is considered that the risk of the subsequent development of generalised MS is low in patients with transverse myelitis.

DEVIC'S DISEASE (NEUROMYELITIS OPTICA)

Neuromyelitis optica is characterised by the development of optic neuritis and spinal cord disease, either simultaneously or rapidly sequentially. The symptoms and signs are similar to the individual disorders described above.

Considerable debate has arisen regarding the relationship between Devic's disease and MS, some feeling that there is a very low conversion rate to generalised disease, whereas others feel that this is simply the initial presentation of what will eventually become generalised MS.

As with other causes of optic neuritis and transverse myelitis, alternative diagnoses should be considered, particularly, in the case of suspected Devic's disease, the possibility of either a localised vasculitis, where the disease is confined to the nervous system, or a generalised vasculitis, where disease outside the nervous system causes signs within the brain.

GENERALISED MULTIPLE SCLEROSIS

Multiple sclerosis is most commonly reported in young adults in Northern Europe, Northern American and Australasia, but is less prevalent towards the equator.

There is strong evidence of a genetic susceptibility to the disorder. The life time risk of developing the disease in Northern Europe is approximately one in 800, which increases to one in 50 for children of affected individuals, and to one in two for siblings of affected individuals. In addition, environmental factors play a part, with an increased risk in people who have been exposed to common childhood viral illness (measles, mumps, rubella and Epstein Barr infection (glandular fever)).

Clinical features

The clinical symptomatology of MS depends upon the site of the neuraxis which is involved. In general, symptoms and signs develop over a period of one to three days, plateau for three to six weeks and then resolve, either completely, to neurological normality, or leaving variable residual disability. In the early stages of the disease, the majority of patients resolve to normality, with increasing residual disability tending to occur in the later stages of the disease.

Although pathological and MR evidence shows that there is considerable involvement of the cerebral white matter, which therefore interrupts information transfer between the major areas of the brain, it is generally considered that this does not result in specific disorders of cognition, for example, language production, verbal understanding, etc. In late stages of the disease, loss of intellectual faculty is well recognised. The evidence for disorders of higher function in the earlier stages of the disease is less compelling.

The majority of patients with MS become depressed. It is difficult to determine whether the depression is a consequence of the diagnosis and the disease burden rather than being a primary event.

One of the commonest manifestations of MS is optic neuritis, the clinical features of which are described above. It is the presenting feature of the disease in 20–25% of patients and will develop during the course of the disease in 50–75% of patients. Some attacks must be subclinical since, pathologically, the optic nerve is involved in all cases.

Disorders of eye movement are particularly common in multiple sclerosis, indicating involvement of the brain stem. Double vision (diplopia) commonly occurs in lateral gaze, to the right or left, due to the presence of either an intranuclear ophthalmoplegia or a lateral rectus palsy. The movement of the eyes as a 'yoked pair' is controlled from the brain stem. The three nerves which move the individual muscles in the eye are linked together, at the nuclear level, by a paired bundle of fibres known as the medial longitudinal bundle. The area of the brainstem containing this bundle is particularly susceptible to attacks of demyelination. When this occurs, the ability of the eyes to move together as a pair is lost, resulting in diplopia to the right or left. The clinical examination reveals a characteristic pattern of eye movement where, on looking to one side or the other, the leading eye does not move fully into the corner of the eye, and develops nystagmus, and the following eye does not cross the mid line. In lateral rectus palsy due to VI nerve involvement, the patient complains of double vision when looking to the affected side. On examination, the eye does not move from the mid-line.

Many patients complain of jerking of the vision in either the horizontal or vertical plane; this is known as oscillopsia, and is the subjective awareness of nystagmus.

When the cerebellar connections are affected, the patient will develop unsteadiness when walking (truncal ataxia), with a wide based gait; there may also be involvement of either or both limbs, leading to clumsiness, particularly manifest in the upper limbs (limb ataxia, formerly known as disdiadokinesis). Speech may become slurred (dysarthria), described by the patients as similar to the effects of excess alcohol.

Affectation of the lower brain stem involving the trigeminal pathways leads to the development of trigeminal neuralgia (see Chapter 1). In general terms, patients with MS develop this at an earlier age than patients with 'idiopathic' trigeminal neuralgia, who, usually, are first symptomatic over the age of 55. However, they require the same investigative procedures as for trigeminal neuralgia in order to exclude a vascular compression, and to confirm that MS is causing the disorder. In all other respects, the symptoms, signs and therapy are the same as for 'idiopathic' trigeminal neuralgia.

Involvement of the spinal cord leads to affectation of the descending motor pathway and the ascending sensory pathway. The commonest level of spinal cord involvement is mid-cervical (C 5/6). Thus, unlike transverse myelitis, which more commonly affects the dorsal spinal cord, and consequently spares the upper limbs, these are almost always involved in cervical disease. The patients complain of diffuse paraesthesia and/or numbness in the hands, associated with loss of dexterity and grip. Depending on the degree of descending motor pathway involvement, there will be increased tone (spasticity) and varying degrees of weakness. Involvement of the sensory pathways from the lower limbs may be confined to the spinothalamic pathways or may include the dorsal columns. It is not unusual to discover signs of cord involvement that the patient has not reported in the history. Patients often do not 'link' the problems in their lower limbs with what is happening in their arms, unless the degree of lower limb involvement is marked. Bladder involvement is also common, particularly in women. Symptomatically, the patients complain of urgency and frequency, which can progress to incontinence. Urodynamic studies (refer to Smith, P, *Urology*, in the Cavendish Medico-Legal Practitioner series) can identify the disorder and differentiate from other bladder affectations. Spinal cord disease is amongst the commoner manifestations of MS, and is often the most debilitating.

Course

In the majority of patients with multiple sclerosis, the disease follows a relapsing/remitting pattern (Figure 8.2). The onset of disease is usually rapid, and the recovery slow; the onset of a relapse can vary between hours and days. The commonly affected sites are the optic nerves, the cervical portion of the spinal cord and the brain stem, and these sites are affected in virtually all patients at some stage of the disease.

The frequency of relapse is variable, some patients having long gaps between relapses, and others having a series of relapses over a short period of time and then a long period in between. In the majority of these patients, with the passage of time, a significant neurological disability is accrued to the point where, usually after a latent interval of 30 years from the onset, the disease becomes secondarily progressive.

There are a small group of patients in whom the disease is progressive from the onset. These typically present with cervical cord disease and the disease is often confined to that area.

In about a fifth of patients, the disease is benign, with long intervals between the relapses, and these patients rarely, if ever, accrue significant neurological disability.

Figure 8.2   Course of different types of multiple sclerosis

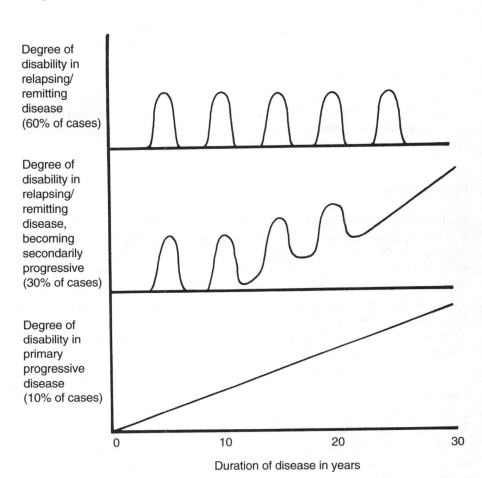

Degree of disability in relapsing/ remitting disease (60% of cases)

Degree of disability in relapsing/ remitting disease, becoming secondarily progressive (30% of cases)

Degree of disability in primary progressive disease (10% of cases)

0   10   20   30

Duration of disease in years

Disability scales are of use in documenting a course of MS and validating the effects of treatment. Most widely used is the expanded disability status scale devised by Kurtske.

Prognosis

The commonest question asked by a patient at the onset of their disease is the long term prognosis. With such a variable disease, this can be very difficult to predict, but purely sensory symptoms and visual symptoms carry a relatively good prognosis, whereas involvement of the motor pathways and the cerebellum carry a poor prognosis. In general, the younger the patient at the time of onset, the better the prognosis, with later onset, particularly in the male, carrying a poor prognosis.

Factors which influence the rate of relapse have been extensively studied. There is evidence that infection can trigger the episode of disease in about a quarter of all patients. In pregnancy, there is evidence that there is a tendency to relapse in the puerperium.

The relationship beyween trauma and multiple sclerosis has been investigated extensively. There is no evidence that trauma will cause MS. The question arises as to whether trauma will precipitate new symptoms, but there is no support for this (Sibley *et al*, 1991).

Investigation

Modern investigation of multiple sclerosis is with evoked potential studies and MR imaging, the latter permitting the exclusion of other disorders which may mimic MS. Evoked potential studies, particularly of the visual pathway, show evidence of any previously unrecognised visual pathway disorders. However, it is important that compressive disease is excluded by imaging.

Analysis of the cerebrospinal fluid by lumbar puncture will, during an acute attack, show evidence of a raised lymphocyte count, and, more particularly, some 85% of patients will show evidence of intrathecal immunoglobulin synthesis (the presence of oligoclonal bands).

Treatment

There is, as yet, no safe or effective cure for multiple sclerosis.

There is good evidence that intravenous methylprednisolone, in high dosage (0.5–1 g daily for three to five days), will shorten the period of time of the relapse, although there is no significant difference in the rate or degree of clinical improvement demonstrated in comparisons between the intramuscular steroids and intravenous steroids. The benefit of intravenous steroids is a marked reduction in significant, immediate or long term adverse effects, even after several courses.

Symptomatic therapy for symptoms is confined to management of the bladder (commonly with oxybutynin at present) and management of paroxysmal painful symptoms (trigeminal neuralgia, paroxysmal sciatica) with anticonvulsants (usually tegretol).

Attempts have been made to influence the long term course of patients with MS using immunosuppressants. There has been widespread support for the use of azathioprine, although there is, as yet, no convincing evidence that such treatment is effective in the long term. Other immunosuppressants can be used and have been shown to be effective (especially cyclosporin), but the side effect profile (nausea, suppression of the bone marrow leading to anaemia) is such that very few patients will tolerate them in the long term.

There has been considerable interest in the use of interferon in the prevention of relapse in patients with MS. There have been, to date, three trials, which appear to show that the rate of relapse may be reduced by a factor of a third. However, the numbers of patients treated have, to date, been small, and the side effect profile of weekly intramuscular injections has been considerable: patients experience flu-like symptoms, pain and, less commonly, skin breakdown (necrosis) at the injection site, and, frequently, significant depression. On this basis, at present there is insufficient evidence to justify its widespread use. Within the European Union, the restrictions on its use (licensed for patients with two or more relapses per year, and without residual neurological disability) are such that, in practice, only a very few patients would qualify. There is no evidence that it has any affect on either stabilising existing disability, or preventing future disability, which are the main concerns of the patient with MS.

CHAPTER 9

TUMOURS

INTRODUCTION

The term, space occupying lesion (SOL), is used to identify any lesion which increases the volume of the intracranial contents and thus leads to a rise in intracranial pressure. This terminology therefore embraces not only intracranial tumours (malignant or benign), but also encompasses vascular lesions and inflammatory lesions (for example, abscess).

PRESENTATION OF INTRACRANIAL TUMOURS

A patient presenting with an SOL requires further investigation to identify the cause of the lesion before this can be termed an intracranial tumour. The manifestations of an intracranial tumour are those of increased intracranial pressure (ICP) and those due to the local effects of the tumour itself. For reasons which are not clearly understood, the signs and symptoms of raised ICP usually pre-date the signs of local disturbance.

The classical triad of raised ICP is headache, papilloedema and vomiting. In one large series, headache was present in 88% of patients, papilloedema in 75% and vomiting in 65%, and all three occurred together in 60%. The headache cause by raised ICP is, at first, usually intermittent. It is described as a throbbing or a bursting pain. It is typically worst first thing in the morning, and wears off within minutes or hours of wakening, and tends to recur towards the end of the day. As the tumour enlarges, the headache becomes more persistent, eventually becoming continuous. The headache is usually increased by any activity which normally raises the intracranial pressure, such as exertion, excitement, coughing, sneezing, vomiting, stooping, intercourse or straining at stool. Some patients find that posture plays a part, the headache being worse when lying down and relieved by sitting up. The headache is usually diffuse and rarely has any localising value. Tumours occurring in the posterior fossa may sometimes initially present with purely occipital headache.

CLINICAL FEATURES OF INTRACRANIAL TUMOURS

Papilloedema is observed with the ophthalmoscope, where there is swelling of the optic nerve head. This can be unilateral, bilateral or asymmetrical, but this has little localising value. When papilloedema is present, the blind spot is, on examination, enlarged, and the peripheral visual fields may show constriction.

If the intracranial pressure is sufficiently elevated, it may be higher than the arterial pressure in the blood vessels to the retina, and hence cause ischaemia. This leads to so called visual obscuration, that is, visual blurring or blindness. Frequently, this occurs with mechanisms which elevate the intracranial pressure such as coughing, straining or stooping.

Vomiting occurs at the time when headache is maximal; initially, this is usually first thing in the morning and towards the end of the day.

Epileptic seizures are due to the direct effect of the tumour on the surrounding or underlying brain. Over the age of 20, about 10% of patients presenting with epilepsy will be found to have an underlying intracranial tumour. Meningiomas (see below, p 131) seem to be particularly liable to cause seizures, which occur in about two thirds of all patients.

With a rapid rise in intracranial pressure, there may be slowing of the heart rate (bradycardia), with an increase in the blood pressure. Respiration in this situation is usually slow and deep.

In the case of chronic raised intracranial pressure, particularly with associated hydrocephalus, the dilatation of the ventricle may erode into the pituitary and cause manifestations of hypopituitarism.

As intracranial pressure rises, the brain may be forced downwards through the tentorium, and this can lead to entrapment of the VI nerve, and occasionally the III nerve. This produces so called 'false localising signs', the cranial nerve palsy being the result of brain swelling rather than direct invasion of the nerve.

The local signs of the tumour depend entirely on its location. Frontal lobe lesions, particularly if bilateral, can lead to a dementing syndrome. Lesions further back, at the motor strip, may lead to weakness down one or other side of the body. Lesions in the temporoparietal cortex on the left can lead to disorders of language, understanding and production, whereas in the right hemisphere, disorders of body image and spatial orientation may occur. Further back, in the occipital lobes, lesions may lead to visual field defects. Lesions in the posterior fossa, particularly involving the cerebellum, may lead to slurred speech (dysarthria) or unsteadiness (ataxia).

The neurological examination is, as always, designed to try and identify the site of the tumour. Assessment of higher intellectual functions may reveal abnormalities as detailed above. In the cranial nerve territory, there may be loss of the sense of smell with olfactory groove meningiomas. The optic fundi will show papilloedema and the visual fields may be abnormal, showing a hemianopic defect. There may be evidence of a III or VI nerve palsy. Abnormalities of facial sensation are unusual. Facial weakness may be part of a cortical lesion (upper motor neurone VII lesion) or reflect direct involvement of the nerve in the posterior fossa (lower motor neurone VII). Hearing may be impaired, particularly in an acoustic neuroma. The lower cranial nerves are rarely involved.

If the tumour involves the motor strip, then there may be evidence of a pyramidal weakness, on one side or the other, with reflex changes comprising hyper-reflexia and, possibly, up-going plantar responses. However, not uncommonly, particularly in slowly growing tumours, examination of the limbs gives normal results, and the plantar response is not a reliable guide to the presence or absence of an intracranial lesion.

Further investigation is then required, either by CT scan or MR scan, which will identify the location of the lesion; increasingly, MR scanning may well also identify the type of the tumour. Biopsy of a lesion may be required prior to attempts at surgical removal.

TYPES OF INTRACRANIAL TUMOUR

Intracranial tumours may be malignant or benign. There is now general agreement that gliomas constitute about 40–45% of all intracranial neoplasms (Figure 9.1), metastases about 20% (Figure 9.5), meningiomas about 10% (Figure 9.2) and acoustic neuromas (Figure 9.3) and pituitary tumours (Figure 9.5) about 5% each.

Gliomas

Gliomas arise from the glial cells. Within the brain, the glial cells form the structural matrix of the brain.

Medulloblastomas

These are rapidly growing tumours which usually occur in the cerebellum, and usually in children. They are occasionally seen in adults. It is the only type of intracranial neoplasm which is known to commonly metastasise to the spinal canal and bone.

Total removal is rarely possible. However, with total or sub total removal and radiotherapy, 10–15 year survival rates are about 40%.

Figure 9.1   MR scan of a brain, showing right temporal glioma

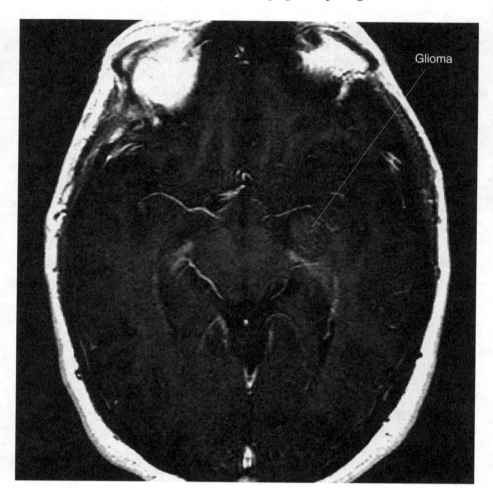

Glioma

Glioblastoma multiforme

This is the most malignant glioma arising in the brain. They tend to occur in middle life. It is usually found in the cerebral hemispheres. These tumours expand rapidly and no form of therapy has, to date, been shown to influence the prognosis, which is universally dire, with survival from diagnosis of three to 12 months.

Astrocytomas

These can occur in any age group, and can occur in either the cerebral or cerebellar hemispheres. They are relatively benign, particularly the childhood form of cerebellar astrocytoma. An average survival after the first symptom is five years for cerebral astrocytomas and 7–8 years for cerebellar astrocytomas.

Oligodendrogliomas

These are slowly growing, usually relatively benign, tumours, occurring in the cerebral hemispheres in young adults. They not uncommonly present as epilepsy, and underline the need for all patients presenting with epilepsy to be investigated with a form of imaging (see Chapter 6).

Given that these tumours are very slowly growing, their detection often presents a dilemma. In a patient whose only symptom is epilepsy, it must be considered whether it is appropriate to undertake major intracranial surgery, with a risk of leaving the patient with a much greater deficit and only incomplete removal of the tumour. If surgery is not going to be offered, the question arises of whether or not the patient should have radiotherapy or chemotherapy. A decision must be made about whether it is appropriate to control the patient's epilepsy, and wait until they have developed signs of other neurological involvement before suggesting surgery.

The decision would be simplified if these tumours were encapsulated, and it could be reliably guaranteed that they could be removed by surgery. However, given that they arise from cells forming part of the matrix of the brain, they are highly infiltrative, and total removal is the exception rather than the rule. Resolution of this dilemma is waiting on improved techniques for differentiating normal from abnormal brain tissue, so that surgical excision can be more precise. Advances in chemotherapy, so that only abnormal tissue is targeted, will potentially develop from research to practice in the next few years.

Ependymomas

These arise from the lining of the ventricles of the brain and, if detected early, are amenable to complete removal. Once they have obliterated the ventricle (particularly the IV), they may then start to infiltrate surrounding brain, so that surgical removal is not as successful.

Meningiomas

These tumours arise from the arachnoid cells which penetrate the dura to form the arachnoid villi; hence, they are attached to the dura. Since they arise from the cells which form the arachnoid villi, they are often found in relationship to the intracranial venous sinuses. Thus, the superior or sagittal sinus gives rise to a parasagittal meningioma; the sphenoparietal sinus and middle meningeal vessels give meningiomas of the sphenoid ridge and the convexities; the olfactory groove of the ethmoid gives rise to olfactory meningioma; and the circle of sinuses around the sella gives rise to suprasellar meningiomas. Meningiomas may occasionally arise from the tentorium, and may be seen in the posterior fossa. Spinal meningiomas, particularly in the thoracic region, are not uncommon.

Meningiomas grow exceedingly slowly, and compress the brain rather than invading it. They can reach prodigious size before clinical presentation (Figure 9.2).

Figure 9.2   MR scan of a brain, showing meningioma

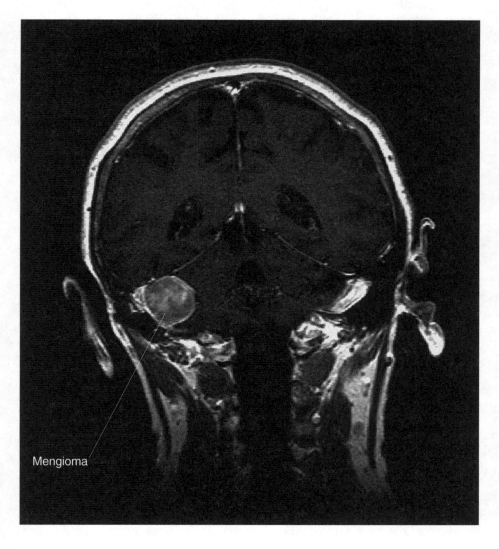

Mengioma

Because of their relationship to the venous sinuses, it is not always possible to completely removal meningiomas surgically. However, their slow rate of growth means that this is rarely of major significance.

Primary malignant lymphomas

Although known lymphomas within the body may produce deposits on the cranial and spinal meninges and present, therefore, as cerebral or spinal compression, lymphomas can arise, however, for the first time in the brain, and are then known as primary malignant lymphomas. The appearance on a CT scan of a solitary lymphoma is very similar to that of a meningioma, and when the lymphomas are multiple, they often appear as multiple metastases. Some forms of lymphoma are particularly sensitive to steroids and, if steroids are given in an attempt to reduce intracranial pressure, repeat scanning 48 hours later may show diminution in the size of the lesion, or it may even appear to have disappeared. These tumours are amenable to chemotherapy and, given that they do not have a distinct scanning appearance, this underlies the need for brain biopsy to identify the tumour type before therapy.

Acoustic neuromas

These are usually unilateral (Figure 9.3). When bilateral, they commonly form part of neurofibromatosis type II. They present as a hearing impairment which is progressive as the tumour expands, and, as the tumor grows out of the auditory canal, it may compress the surrounding exiting cranial nerves and, with further extent, impinge on the pons (cerebral pontine angle syndrome). Although rare, neuromas can arise from other cranial nerves, typically II and V.

Figure 9.3   MR of a brain, showing an acoustic neuroma

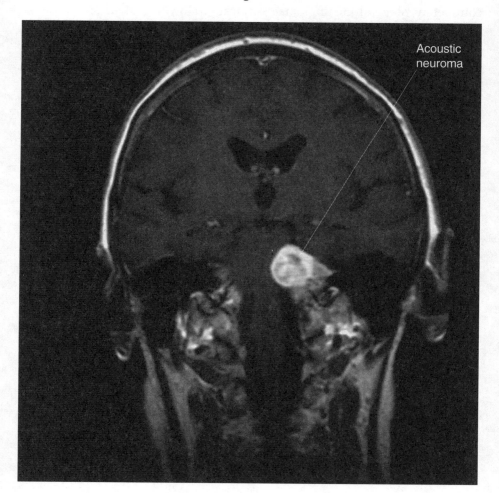

Acoustic
neuroma

Craniopharyngiomas

These are tumours arising from embryonic remnants which fail to completely resorb during embryonic life. They are very slow growing tumours. They grow upwards from above the sella turcica into the third ventricle and hypothalamus, and may extend up between the hemispheres and cause compression. They are amenable to surgery.

Pituitary tumours

These tumours arise within the pituitary itself, and are defined as secreting and non-secreting adenomas. Secreting adenomas release excessive hormones into the circulation, and may be identified from their systemic effect. The tumour grows locally within the pituitary fossa, expands it, and may extend through the sella turcica into the area of the optic chiasm, and neurological presentation may, therefore, be by the detection of visual field defects.

Many of the secreting adenomas are amenable to drug therapy, and do not, therefore, require surgery. Most non-secreting adenomas require surgical removal.

Figure 9.4   MR scan of a brain, showing large pituitary tumour

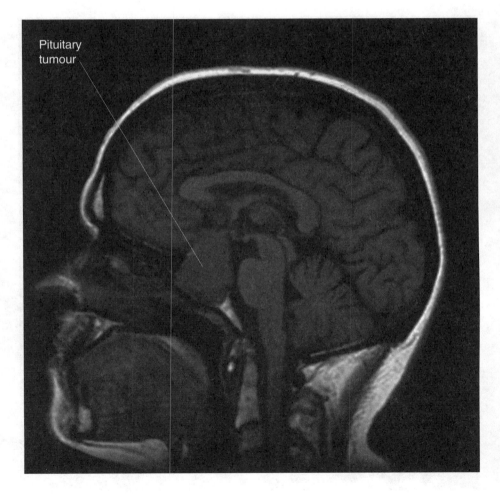

Pituitary
tumour

Metastatic tumours

Some 25% of intracerebral neoplasms are secondary to a primary growth elsewhere, usually lung, breast, stomach, kidney or thyroid. In the 55+ age group, metastatic tumour is more common than primary intracranial tumour.

In general, the outlook for patients with intracranial tumour is improving since diagnosis has been greatly simplified by the advent, initially, of CT scanning and, more recently, MR scanning. Tumours are therefore identified when they are of smaller size, which facilitates surgical intervention. Any patient presenting with a history suggestive of raised ICP or of focal neurological deficit requires detailed neurological examination and investigation to identify the cause.

Figure 9.5   MR scan of a brain, showing metastatic tumour

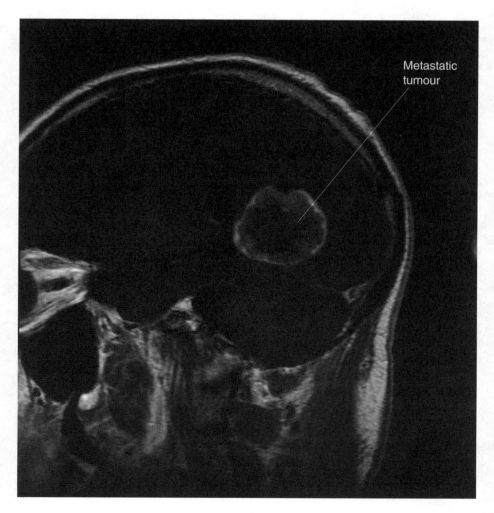

Metastatic tumour

CHAPTER 10

HEADACHE

INTRODUCTION

Headache is amongst the commonest symptoms described by patients to their general practitioners, and some 20% of males and 50% of females describe headache on a least one day each week. It is always important to ask the patient to describe what they mean by headache, since no two patients have the same perception of a headache. A patient presenting with headache requires careful consideration of the history, and may well require investigation.

With respect to the history and symptoms, the patient must be questioned in order to determine:

(a) how long he or she has suffered from a headache;

(b) what words best describe the headache, for example, throbbing, pounding, stabbing, knife-like, bursting or aching;

(c) whether the headache is increasing in severity, or is static or improving;

(d) whether the headache is constant or comes and goes;

(e) at what time of the day, if the headache is paroxysmal, the headache comes on;

(f) whether there are any factors which regularly relieve the headache, and whether there are any special circumstances which the patient avoids that increases the headache;

(g) whether the headache is associated with any disturbance of vision (visual obscuration, double vision);

(h) whether there is any vomiting or nausea;

(i) whether there is any local tenderness in the scalp;

(j) whether there has been any recent head injury or symptoms suggestive of sinus disease;

(k) whether there is any history suggestive of cervical spondylotic disease;

(l) whether the patient is taking any drugs which are known to cause headache; and

(m) whether the patient has recently been anxious or depressed.

Examination in the majority of patients with headache will be entirely normal and the diagnosis, therefore, rests on the history. In patients where neurological examination shows an abnormality, further investigation, including scanning modalities, are indicated.

Headaches associated with intracranial tumours and vascular disease are dealt with in the appropriate chapters, as are headaches following head injury.

MIGRAINE

There is perhaps more confusion surrounding the diagnosis of migraine than that of any other headache type. Patients and their medical attendants will often ascribe a headache to migraine even though it does not have any of the characteristics of the condition and, hence, the value of the word has been diminished.

Patients who suffer from migraine, as defined, will almost all, in their own words, give a similar story. The former classification into classical migraine and common migraine has been replaced, with classical migraine now being called migraine with aura, and common migraine being called migraine without aura.

Some 70% of patients who suffer from migraine have a family history of the condition, and one rare form of migraine (familiar hemiplegic migraine) has now been shown to have an associated gene abnormality.

The majority of migrainers are aware, sometime in the 24 hours preceding the onset of their attack, that an episode is about to occur. Frequently they feel excessively tired, they may yawn excessively and many patients experience a craving for a particular type of food. Also, many patients have a feeling of heightened awareness, in that they feel that they could tackle more in that 24 hours than they could in the rest of the week put together. Fluid retention may occur, particularly in the female.

In patients who have migraine with aura, this aura ushers in the migraine attack proper. The aura is usually visual, with so called visual scintillations occurring in one or other hemifield. There may be visual scotomata (partial loss of the visual field – see Chapter 8, Figure 8.1), and some patients develop frank tunnel vision. This can be associated with, or occur independently from, episodes of numbness on the side of the face, the side of the tongue and the arm, and some patients may experience disturbance of speech comprehension or production. Commonly, the aura lasts between 15 minutes and an hour and then disappears. With patients experiencing an aura for the first time, they commonly believe that they are developing a stroke.

There is usually an interval between the termination of the aura and the onset of the headache phase. The headache can be one sided (hemicranial), generalised, anterior or posterior. It can spread on to the face and into the neck. It usually gains slowly in intensity and is associated with nausea and, in some patients, vomiting. It is associated with intolerance of light, the patient preferring a darkened room, intolerance of noise, the patient preferring to be quiet, and intolerance of smell, where the thought or smell of food is likely to induce waves of nausea. The symptoms are sufficiently severe to take the patient out of their situation, and the majority of patients take to their beds for the duration of the headache phase, which can be anything from 6–72 hours. During the day following the migraine attack, patients feel 'washed out' with the obverse of the prodrome, with appetite suppression, variable feelings of heightened or lowered perception and, in females who have had fluid retention, marked diuresis. From this, it can be seen that a patient who says, 'I have a migraine every day, doctor,' cannot be described as having a true migraine.

Given that migraine is inherited in a large proportion of patients, the concept of a trigger, which will convert the underlying tendency formally into the active disease, is now well established. The trigger can be emotional, physical or a combination of both.

The majority of patients with migraine start developing their attacks in their late teens through to their late 20s. Emotional factors such as the death of a grandparent, the death of a family pet, examination stress and puberty are well recognised triggers. In terms of trauma, the most common trigger is minor head trauma following, for example, an accidental blow to the head against an open cupboard door. Migraine may develop for the first time following whiplash. Such triggering events can be determined in about 75% of all migrainers.

Triggers to the individual attack, although much discussed, are not as common as supposed. In about 25% of patients, the attack may be triggered by chocolate, cheese, marmite and citrus fruits. However, a much commoner trigger to the individual attack is disruption in the pattern of sleeping and of eating.

In the female, migraine attacks may be more frequent at the time of the menses, and there is a rare form of migraine (catamenial migraine) where attacks only occur at menstruation.

Management is by explanation to the patient of the nature of the condition and reassurance that they do not have any sinister underlying neurological disease. With some patients, this requires imaging of the brain. Patients are encouraged to avoid their own known triggers, and treatment is then designed for the individual attack to lessen the symptoms of that attack, along with prophylaxis to prevent further attacks developing.

CLUSTER HEADACHE

This condition is much more of a problem in the male than in the female, with a ratio of about 6:1. As the name suggests, the patient tends to get clusters of attacks occurring over a defined period and then long periods of relief. During the attack, the pain is in and around the eye. It is associated, in the majority of patients, with reddening of the eye, increased lacrimation from the eye, increased nasal secretion and, sometimes, changes in the pupil size and shape; Occasionally, the patient will also experience pins and needles immediately above the eye lid.

In contradistinction to patients with migraine, the pain of a cluster headache is sufficiently severe that often a patient will attempt to provide counter pressure by banging the head against the wall. The severe pain lasts anything from 30 minutes to three hours and then subsides. Typically, the patient is woken from sleep at their first period of rapid eye movement sleep, usually between 2 and 4 in the morning, and, if the attacks recur, they tend to recur 12 hours later, in the early part of the afternoon. A typical cluster interval is three months, with a spread from one to five months.

Patients with cluster headaches have their attacks triggered by smoking and by alcohol, and most patients have learned to avoid these precipitants before the diagnosis has been established.

Occasionally, patients may have more than one cluster episode per annum, and there is a rare condition, known as chronic cluster, where the patient has intermittent attacks throughout the year without any definite clustering.

Treatment for the individual attack is by rebreathing pure oxygen, and some of the drugs currently used in the treatment of migraine are effective if given intramuscularly.

TENSION HEADACHE

Tension headache, otherwise known as muscle contraction headache, is amongst the commonest forms of headache experienced and is usually associated with episodes of stress.

Patients feel that they have a tight, band-like sensation around the head up to the vertex. This is usually present daily and for most of the day, and tends to get worse as the day goes on. In contradistinction to migraine, however, it does not take the patient out of their situation and there is no associated nausea, vomiting, photophobia, phonophobia or osmophobia.

Many patients with tension headache develop into a chronic phase. Since their anxiety that they have structural underlying brain pathology is enhanced by lack of understanding of the condition, many such patients require imaging of the brain to relieve their anxieties before treatment can be instituted.

With both migraine and tension headache, the concept of chronic daily headache as a consequence of analgesia abuse is now recognised. In both conditions, increasing dependence on 'over the counter' analgesic preparations increases the frequency of either the tension headache or the migraine and, hence, the frequency of the use of simple analgesics. It has been estimated that two simple analgesics daily over a period of six weeks will induce headache in a previously non headache prone individual. Getting patients off routine analgesia will improve the headache in the vast majority.

BENIGN INTRACRANIAL HYPERTENSION

Although it is described as 'benign', patients sometimes experience consequences which are far from benign. The condition is that of the headache which has all the features of raised intracranial pressure (see Chapter 5), with an early morning headache wearing off as the day goes on, the headache being increased by coughing, stooping and straining, and the subsequent development of visual obscurations. On examination, the patients will be shown to have papilledema.

Although benign intracranial hypertension (BIH) may be due to structural pathology within the brain (see Chapter 7), it is more often idiopathic, that is, no cause can be found, or it may be associated with pregnancy or obesity. It is important that all patients presenting in such a manner receive detailed neurological investigations to exclude a more sinister cause.

In patients with BIH, there is frequently colour desaturation (the patient seeing all in front of them as grey) indicating a high degree of intracranial pressure. Although, for the majority of patients, the disease is self-limiting and responds to treatment with carbonic anhydrase inhibitors, for some patients, particularly those who develop colour desaturation, they may require optic nerve fenestration to bring their condition under control.

CHAPTER 11

NEUROLOGICAL INFECTIONS

ACUTE PURULENT MENINGITIS

Introduction

The brain and spinal cord are covered by three membranes (meninges), named, from outside to in, the dura mater, the arachnoid mater and the pia mater.

The dura mater is a thick fibrous structure and is closely applied to the inside of the skull. Folds of the dura separate the cranial cavity into its compartments, these being the falx cerebri (separating the right hemisphere from the left hemisphere), the tentorium (separating the cortex from the posterior fossa) and the falx cerebeli (separating the cerebellar hemispheres).

The arachnoid mater lies between the dura and the pia and bridges over the sulci of the brain. The space between the arachnoid and pia (subarachnoid space) contains the cerebrospinal fluid (CSF). The pia mater is a delicate membrane which lies over the surface of the brain.

A pyogenic meningitis is a medical emergency. Despite advances in antibiotic therapy and improvements in general management, mortality rates have not improved significantly over this last 30–40 years.

The commonest bacterial species producing meningitis are the neisseria meningitides, streptococcus pneumoniae and haemophilus influenza type B. In patients who are immunocompromised, unusual bacterial pathogens are frequently the cause of meningitis, many of which are nosocomial (acquired in hospital).

Recurrent bacterial meningitis is usually due to a fracture of the skull secondary to head injury, the most common site of that fracture being through the cribriform plate at the ethmoid leading to communication between the subarachnoid space and the nasopharynx.

The bacteria causing meningitis enters the subarachnoid space predominantly via the blood stream. The immediate source of the bacteria for the common causes of meningitis (haemophilus influenza, meningococci or pneumococci) is the nasopharynx. The reasons why the bacteria then spreads from the nasopharynx into the blood supply and, hence, to the brain are ill understood.

Clinical features

The clinical features of meningitis are, initially, those of an upper respiratory tract infection accompanied by a feeling of illness, weakness, myalgia (muscle pain) and sometimes backache. In a variable period, ranging from hours to days, the signs of inflammation of the meninges themselves start to predominate with the well recognised triad of headache, photophobia and muscle spasm. By this stage the patient usually has a detectable increase in body core temperature (pyrexia).

The headache is usually described as severe, and sometimes bursting, in character and is steadily progressive. It is made worse by movement and is usually associated with nausea and vomiting.

Spinal muscle spasm is evoked by attempting to flex the spine, producing a variable degree of neck rigidity. Kernig's sign would be variably positive, that is, there would be pain when attempting to extend the knee with the hip flexed. Attempting to flex the neck may produce flexion of the hips and knees (Bradzinski's sign).

From early in the course of the disease, there is usually a degree of impairment of mental faculties, ranging from drowsiness, through to coma in fulminant disease. The progression of meningitis is variable and unpredictable. About a third of patients will have associated seizures. They may occur at any stage of the illness, though they are rarely a presenting feature.

As the meningitis develops, so does cerebral oedema and it is the development of the latter which leads to coma. If tentorial herniation occurs, there may be false localising cranial nerve palsies and, in severe cases, there may be brain stem distortion. This can lead to disturbance of respiration.

Petechial rash is seen in about 60% of patients suffering from meningococcal meningitis, although, in the early stages of the disease, it may be very scattered and difficult to detect.

Since the organism enters the brain via the blood, the associated bacteremia may produce its own complications, particularly in meningococcal meningitis, when disseminated intravascular coagulation can occur.

Post meningitic sequelae occur in about 20% of cases, ranging from deafness as an isolated finding, through to severe brain damage.

Investigation

The diagnosis is achieved via a blood culture and lumbar puncture, the latter being the most important. Depending on the timing of the lumbar puncture, the CSF may vary, from being only mildly abnormal, through to frank pus. If there is any evidence of focal neurological abnormality, some form of imaging (computerised tomography/magnetic resonance) should be undertaken prior to the lumbar puncture.

Once the CSF has been examined, then immediate therapy with antibiotics is mandatory. Even if an organism cannot be identified immediately in the CSF, the use of broad spectrum antibiotics to cover against the three common causes of meningitis should be instituted.

There is considerable debate as to whether the use of steroids modifies the outcome in patients with meningitis. However, if there is evidence of cerebral oedema, then most physicians would favour its use.

Inappropriate antidiuretic hormone (ADH) secretion, leading to hypomatremia, may develop in any patient with meningitis, usually in the first three days, and this needs to be specifically looked for and, if it develops, treated with water restriction.

SPECIFIC TYPES OF MENINGITIS

Meningococcal meningitis

There has been a marked change in the epidemiology of meningitis in the United Kingdom and other parts of Europe because of an increase in type 15 strains. This has been particularly noted in teenagers. The organism probably spreads from person to person via the respiratory route. However, some 20% of the 'normal' population will carry meningococci in the nasopharynx and are not affected. The reason why teenagers are particularly at risk of progressing from an innocent carriage of meningococcus to developing meningitis is not understood.

Four types of meningococcal sepsis have been identified:

(a) bacteraemia: this presents with mild symptoms only;

(b) meningococcaemia: in this situation, the patient is ill, has a typical rash and has disseminated vascular coagulation, but no meningitis;

(c) meningitis: in this situation, the patient has no focal signs and variable levels of consciousness;

(d) meningeal encephalitis: patients present with meningeal signs, together with profound changes in consciousness and evidence of widespread cerebral dysfunction.

A predominant feature of meningococcal meningitis is the rash, which most frequently starts as small (1–2 mm) petechiae on the pressure areas of the body, on the trunk or the legs. These petechiae can coalesce to form ecchymoses of variable sizes. They are seen in between 50% and 86% of cases.

Disseminated intravascular coagulation is a major feature of the disease due to Gram negative shock. This is the development of endotoxic shock, which leads to the rapid death of many patients with meningococci meningitis. Evidence of cardiac involvement (myocarditis) is seen, especially in those with the severe form of the disease. A small, but significant, number of patients will go on to develop a pericarditis or arthritis. Treatment for meningococcal meningitis is with penicillin in appropriate doses. This usually leads to resolution of the pyrexia and the associated headache and neck stiffness over a period of six days. The treatment of the Gram negative shock has been greatly improved by plasmapheresis which removes the toxic elements from the blood.

Mortality from meningococcal meningitis is between 5% and 10%. Older patients and those in poor socio-economic circumstances have been associated with the highest mortality. In a study of 86 deaths from meningococcal meningitis in the United Kingdom, in 71 cases, a delay in diagnosis directly contributed to the death, suggesting that a high index of suspicion must always be maintained.

Contacts of patients with proven meningococcal meningitis should be treated with rifampicin, since their risk of developing the disease increases by about 500 fold. Vaccines against meningitis, mainly meningococcal meningitis, are now becoming available.

Haemophilus influenza meningitis

This is predominantly a disease of infants and young children, 92% of cases occurring under the age of four. The onset of the clinical features is usually less dramatic than other forms of meningitis, and lethargy and mild evidence of meningeal irritation may be the early symptoms. It may take up to 48 hours for signs of cerebral irritation to develop. Otherwise, management is as for any other form of meningitis.

Pneumococcal meningitis

This, in the adult, tends to be a disease of the over 50s, and often results from bacteremia secondary to a focus of infection in the lungs, the ear or the sinuses. About a third of patients overall will have had a pneumonia. The onset of fulminant meningeal symptoms is often very rapid, occurring over a few hours.

Mortality in adults with pneumococcal disease is high, at about 50%, but this may reflect high incidence of associated disease. Treatment is with penicillin.

Acute lymphocytic meningitis

The clinical features of viral meningitis are similar, irrespective of the virus causing the illness. There is usually sudden intense headache, fever and neck stiffness, associated with variable degrees of drowsiness or confusion. Evidence of cerebral involvement is not part of the viral meningitis picture. Malaise listlessness, myalgia, nausea and vomiting are frequently present. In general terms, the patients do not look as ill as those with bacterial meningitis. The symptoms usually resolve within a few days and most patients are well within a fortnight. Long term neurological sequelae are not common. The common viruses are the coxsackie virus, echo virus and mumps.

Chronic meningitis

The majority of patients with a chronic meningitis will develop their symptoms over a period of seven days, although the course can be similar for acute purulent meningitis. In the immunocompetent individual, the most important cause is tuberculous meningitis. In the immunocompromised individual, fungal infections assume greater importance.

Tuberculous meningitis

In the days before specific antibiotic therapy was available for tuberculous meningitis, the disease was described as the great 'mimic', in that virtually any combination of neurological symptoms or signs could be produced by the disease. In the early stages of the disease, the patient is often apathetic, irritable, anorexic and restless. Subsequently, they become confused and show abnormal behaviour to the point that some patients initially present to the psychiatric department. Convulsions may occur and cranial nerve palsies, particularly III, IV and VII, develop due to affectation of the basal meninges. Untreated, the disease progresses to coma and death within four to six weeks. Tuberculoses may develop in the brain or the spinal cord as part of the meningitis or subsequent to its treatment.

Diagnosis depends on identification of the tubercule baccilli in the CSF with appropriate staining.

BRAIN ABSCESS

Brain abscesses present as a combination of signs of raised intracranial pressure with focal neurological signs. The progression is usually over one to two weeks. Previously, when the incidence of suppurative ear disease was high, the commonest cause was spread from an infected ear. Nowadays, they more commonly result from trauma. The frontal and temporal lobes of the brain are most likely to be involved.

The patient will present with evolving focal neurological deficit, sometimes associated with seizure activity. These symptoms and signs then evolve into those of raised intracranial pressure, with headache, nausea and vomiting, and the progressive clouding of consciousness to coma. The patient may present with the signs of raised intracranial pressure initially and then develop evidence of focal neurological deficit.

The single most important investigation is brain imaging (CT/MRI) (Figure 11.1). Lumbar punctures should not be undertaken, since this would inevitably cause deterioration due to herniation.

Figure 11.1   MR scan of a brain, showing left parietal abcess

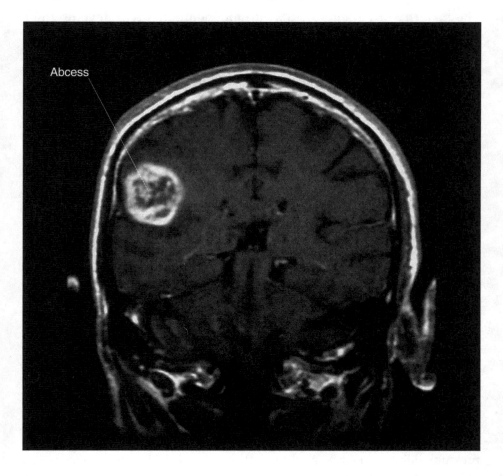

Previously, surgical expiration of the abscess was the treatment modality of choice. However, if the source of the infection can be identified, then, along with appropriate antibiotic therapy, the patient's condition can be monitored by serial scanning which may obviate the need for surgical intervention. However, in most centres a combination of surgery and antibiotic treatment is the preferred approach.

The mortality of cerebral abscesses has decreased to about 10%. However, neurological sequelae can be severe in terms of epilepsy, neurological deficit and intellectual changes. Epilepsy is more likely to occur in the younger patient and if seizures were present at the time of presentation. Given the high risk of epilepsy, prophylactic anticonvulsant medication has been suggested for up to five years after treatment for the abscess.

Focal neurological deficit, in terms of hemiparesis, persists in between 25% and 50% of patients and are predicted by the level of consciousness and the presence of focal neurological deficit at onset. In general, the more severe the neurological presentation, the more likely there will be a focal deficit.

Changes in higher intellectual functions occur in the vast majority of patients who have had raised intracranial pressure, and need to be formally identified by a neuropsychologist.

ACUTE ENCEPHALITIS

The distinction between acute meningitis and encephalitis is not always clear cut. In patients with encephalititis, the emphasis of the disease is on the cortex, and the signs of meningeal irritation are less marked. Changes in consciousness range from obtundation through to deep coma, and there is usually considerable disorganisation of speech comprehension and production, personality and orientation. Focal neurological deficit (commonly hemiparesis) and seizures frequently co-exist.

Although there are numerous causes of encephalitis, the commonest in the United Kingdom and Europe is herpes simplex encephalitis. This is a rare complication of infection by the herpes simplex virus, occurring in between one and three per million of the population. The virus has a predilection for the temporal lobes and, to a lesser extent, the frontal lobes, which determines the clinical picture. There is usually an abrupt onset of fever, headache and vomiting, and decreased level of consciousness and seizures are common in the early stages. Progression to coma is usually rapid over a few days. The fronto-temporal involvement leads to bizarre behaviour patterns with disorientation and sometimes severe memory loss; hallucinations, particularly auditory or olfactory, are frequent, and aphasia, reflecting damage to the posterior parts of the temporal lobe, is common. With progression, there is evidence of evolving hemiparesis and visual field disorders. As the disease progresses, the signs of increased intracranial pressure develop and become the dominant clinical feature.

The mortality of untreated herpes simplex encephalitis is extremely high, and those patients who are comatosed at the time of presentation usually die. The herpes virus may be identified in the CSF directly by molecular techniques, and treatment is with intravenous acyclovir. As noted previously, the risk of long term neurological sequelae is high.

CHAPTER 12

NERVE AND NEUROMUSCULAR JUNCTION DISORDERS

DISORDERS OF THE PERIPHERAL NERVES AND PLEXUSES

Diseases of the peripheral nerves can be divided into those which are generalised (polyneuropathy) or those which are confined to the territory of a single nerve (mononeuropathy). Polyneuropathy can be further sub divided on the basis of nerve conduction studies and electromyographs (EMGs) into those which predominantly affect the myelin (demyelinating neuropathies) (see Chapter 1, Figure 1.2) and those which predominantly affect the axon (axonal neuropathies).

The clinical features of a neuropathy are those of motor symptoms and signs and sensory symptoms and signs. Weakness is the commonest motor symptom, and is usually associated with a degree of wasting of the affected muscle, and absent tendon reflexes in the muscle concerned. Weakness which begins symmetrically and peripherally in the lower limbs implies a diffuse and generalised peripheral neuropathy, whereas when the weakness is confined to the distribution of a single peripheral nerve or motor root, damage to that particular nerve or root is implied. In general, muscle wasting is indicative of long standing neuropathies.

Sensory symptoms can be divided into those which are positive, due to irritation of the nerve, and those which are negative, due to loss of function. Positive sensory symptoms comprise paraesthesiae (pins and needles) and dysesthesiae (painful, burning pins and needles). These sensations are usually unpleasant and are increased by stimulation (hyperaesthesiae).

The most common negative sensory symptom is that of loss of sensation, or numbness. In a generalised neuropathy, this usually starts at the toes and ascends to the upper calves; it then begins to involve the fingers and spreads up the arm, resulting in the classic 'glove and stocking' distribution of sensory loss characteristic of a peripheral neuropathy. A less common negative sign is due to loss of proprioception, where the patient is unable to locate accurately the position of the feet and hands in space, complaining of unsteadiness on walking and clumsiness of the hands. When severe, there may appear to be a tremor of the hands as the wrists go through an increased range of movement to enable the individual to recognise where their hands are in space.

If the autonomic system is involved, then patients complain of loss of sweating, and develop orthostatic hypotension (fall in blood pressure when achieving the upright posture).

An abbreviated classification of the neuropathies is given below:

(a) inherited neuropathies;

(b) acute acquired neuropathies;

(c) sub acute acquired neuropathies;

(d) chronic acquired neuropathies;

(e) relapsing neuropathies;

(f) mononeuropathies (cranium and limb); and

(g) mononeuritis multiplex.

Inherited neuropathies

These are now classified as hereditary motor sensory neuropathies, types I–VII. Types I and II (formerly known as Charcot-Marie tooth (CMT) disease or peroneal muscular atrophy (PMA)) are by far the commonest, being, respectively, the demyelinating and axonal forms of inherited neuropathies. These conditions are present from birth, the classical finding being that of *pes cavus* due to weakness of the intrinsic muscles of the foot; there may also be weakness of the intrinsic muscles of the hand. In type I, the peripheral nerves are often thickened and nerve conduction studies show a marked slowing of conduction.

Inheritance is autosomal dominant, but variability of expression occurs within families. This has been shown to be due to the extent of the gene defect. The smaller that extent, the less severe the clinical expression, while with a greater degree of gene disruption the clinical manifestations become more severe. Management is entirely symptomatic.

Acute acquired neuropathies

The commonest acute acquired neuropathy is Guillain-Barré syndrome. This commonly follows a viral infection but can be seen with bacterial infections, particularly helicobacter. It can occur following vaccinations and has been reported following streptokinase therapy for myocardial infarction. In about one third of cases, no antecedent cause is identified.

Patients present with weakness starting in the feet and ascending through the legs, involving the muscles of respiration and the upper limbs. The evolution can be over a period of days (up to 14) or over a matter of hours. Patients often complain of sensory disturbance, but no objective abnormality of sensation is found on examination. Occasionally, the cranial nerves are involved but there is, however, a rare variant of Guillain-Barré syndrome (Miller-Fisher syndrome) which presents with cranial nerve involvement, comprising ophthalmoplegia and ataxia.

Investigation with nerve conduction studies shows slowing of conduction in the peripheral nerves. Lumbar puncture shows an increased protein which is, in the majority of cases, without any cellular response.

Because of the risk of respiratory involvement, all patients should be in hospital on a unit with access to intensive care. Serial measurement of peak flow may give warning of impending respiratory impairment and, in most units, patients with a peak flow of less than 100 l/min would be electively ventilated. Some 25% of patients develop cardiac dysrhythmias associated with respiratory failure.

There are two modalities of treatment which are now standard practice, iv globulin therapy and plasmapheresis. With appropriate therapy, some 75% of patients will make a virtually complete recovery and will be left with no residual disability. In 25% of patients, there will be residual disability ranging from mild to moderate.

Porphyria

In acute intermittent porphyria, a metabolic disorder, a picture very similar to Guillain-Barré syndrome may develop, porphyria being the major differential diagnosis of the Guillain-Barré syndrome.

Sub acute acquired neuropathies

In these patients, the neuropathy develops over a period of weeks or months, and most are due to deficiency states, toxin, metabolic disturbance or inflammatory conditions. The patient usually complains initially of dysesthesiae, particularly in the feet, gradually spreading upwards to the knees and then involving the fingers and hands. The weakness develops late in the course of the clinical picture.

The commonest condition producing a sub acute acquired neuropathy is diabetes mellitus. Although over 60% of patients with diabetes will show electrical evidence of a peripheral neuropathy, only about 30% are symptomatic. The neuropathy is time dependent and, the longer the patient has the disease, the more likely they are to develop evidence of neuropathy. In addition to a symmetrical polyneuropathy, patients with diabetes may also develop mononeuritis multiplex, autonomic neuropathy, entrapment neuropathies and femoral neuropathy.

Other causes of sub acute acquired neuropathies are alcohol, arsenic, lead, industrial solvents (particularly benhexane) and drugs (antibiotics, anticonvulsants, antirheumatics, cytotoxics, cardiovascular drugs).

Chronic acquired neuropathies

In these patients, the symptoms arise over months or years, but are otherwise similar to sub acute neuropathies. Chronic neuropathies are associated with carcinomas with paraproteinaemia, B1 deficiency, connective tissue disorders and amyloid.

Relapsing neuropathies

Patients who have undergone an episode of Guillain-Barré syndrome may have a secondary relapse. In this situation, treatment is less successful than in the primary event. Porphyria is probably the commonest form of a relapsing neuropathy, particularly in relation to inappropriate drug treatment.

In general, it has been estimated that 20–30% of patients will never have the cause of their neuropathy identified at the time of first presentation. If symptoms persist, then the patient should be re-evaluated at intervals.

Mononeuropathies

Cranial mononeuropathies

Spinal accessory nerve

After the nerve becomes extracranial, the spinal portion of the spinal accessory nerve descends into the neck, close to the internal jugular vein. It then passes deep into, and innervates, the sternomastoid muscle and comes through the posterior border of that muscle at the junction of the upper and the middle third. It then passes obliquely into the posterior triangle of the neck to reach the upper trapezius muscle, which it innervates.

In the posterior triangle, the nerve is vulnerable and can be irreparably damaged by radiation, or ressected during radical neck dissections. These are recognised side effects rather than complications. However, they are more commonly injured at the transverse of the posterior triangle of the neck during minor surgical procedures such as biopsy or excision of lymph nodes and other small masses.

As a consequence of damage to the nerve, the trapezius muscle loses its innervation and there is drooping of the shoulder and weakness of shoulder innervation.

Upper limb mononeuropathies

Long thoracic nerve (of Bell)

This nerve is derived from the 5th, 6th and 7th cervical roots and supplies the serratus anterior muscle. This fixes the scapula to the chest wall, and weakness causes winging of the scapula. The nerve is injured alone most frequently as a result of pressure on the shoulder, and occasionally follows an infective illness.

Radial nerve

The radial nerve is a continuation of the posterior cord of the brachial plexus, and innervates the extensor group of muscles of the wrist and fingers and the triceps. It also provides sensation to the lower half of the radial aspect of the arm, and onto the dorsum of the hand. Damage to the radial nerve above the elbow produces wrist and finger drop, with sensory loss. The nerve is most vulnerable to damage in the spiral groove of the humerus. Compression of the radial nerve is the classic cause of 'Saturday night palsy', where the nerve is compressed as an intoxicated individual falls asleep with the arm extended over the arm of a chair. Less common injuries are misplaced injections and malpositioning of a patient during anaesthesia.

Median nerve

This is formed by the union of the two heads from the inner and outer cords of the brachial plexus. In the forearm, it supplies the flexors of the wrist and fingers, and impairment of function therefore leads to weakness of grip and sensory loss, usually over the thumb, index and middle finger. The median nerve may be compressed at the elbow by the pronator teres muscle. At that site, it is also vulnerable to diagnostic or therapeutic punctures in the antecubital fossa. These include venepuncture and infusions, and arterial punctures, usually for blood gas measurement and cardiac catheterisation.

Entrapment at the wrist is commonly due to the carpal tunnel syndrome and occurs spontaneously, predominantly in women and during pregnancy. It is also seen following fractures, in association with acromegaly and hypothyroidism. It can develop after the formation of a fistula for haemodialysis in renal failure.

Ulnar nerve

The ulnar nerve is derived from the 8th cervical and 1st thoracic spinal nerves. It lies behind the medial condyle of the humerus at the elbow, and supplies the muscles which flex the wrist on the ulnar side. In the hand, it supplies most of the small muscles.

Damage to the nerve at the elbow causes weakness of grip in the ulnar side of the hand and wasting of the first dorsal interosseus muscle. Sensory loss is in the ring and little fingers, extending up to the wrist. Damage occurring at the elbow may occur from repeated minor trauma, for example, in patients who drive their car with their elbow resting on the window or who sit at their desks for long periods propped on their elbows. It may also be due to metabolic causes, particularly diabetes.

The iatrogenic ulnar neuropathies occur peri-operatively, in which situation, about 10% are bilateral. They occur more frequently in the male and in thin or obese individuals rather than normal individuals. Most are attributed to arm positioning at the time of surgery.

At the wrist, the ulnar nerve may be injured by cuts, and the median nerve may be involved at the same time. A pressure neuropathy of the deep palmar branch of the ulnar nerve can occur occupationally in individuals who have prolonged or recurrent pressure on the outer part of the palm.

Lower limb mononeuropathies

Femoral nerve

The femoral nerve is derived from the lumbar plexus. It forms in the psoas muscle, passes through the pelvis and enters the thigh beneath the inguinal ligament, lateral to the femoral sheath and femoral vessels. Infra-abdominally, it sends branches to the iliacus muscle and, in the femoral triangle, it divides into the terminal branches supplying sartorius and quadriceps. The sensory branches of the nerve supply the anterior and medial aspects of the thigh in its lower two thirds, and the saphenous branch supplies sensation to the inner aspect of the leg and the foot.

The major clinical abnormality in femoral nerve palsy is weakness of knee extension due to paralysis of the quadriceps. The leg gives way when walking or climbing stairs and when getting out of a chair. There is loss of sensation in the cutaneous innervation of the nerve.

Femoral neuropathies can be caused by an abscess in the psoas muscle, by a haematoma in the iliacus muscle or by pelvic neoplasia. The femoral nerve can be damaged in fractures of the pelvis or the femur, or by hip dislocation or replacement. Most of the injuries are caused by stretching of the nerve, particularly by retractors.

Investigation is with nerve conduction studies to confirm the neuropathy. Mass lesions in the pelvis are best identified by ultrasound.

Sciatic nerve

The sciatic nerve leads from the sacral plexus, deriving its nerve roots from the 4th and 5th lumbar and the 1st, 2nd and 3rd sacral spinal roots. The nerve runs through the pelvis by way of the sciatic notch into the buttock and then descends in the back of the thigh. Close to the popliteal fossa, it divides into the common peroneal and tibial nerves.

In the thigh, the nerve supplies the hamstring muscles and, via the common peroneal and tibial nerves, supplies all of the muscles beneath the knee. With complete interruption of the sciatic nerve, there is paralysis of flexion of the knee and all the muscles beneath the knee. Foot drop occurs as a result of paralysis of the anterior tibial group of muscles and the peronei, hence, patients drag the toes of the affected foot and are unable to stand on their toes. Sensory loss is over the outer and lower aspect of the lower leg and across the dorsum of the foot.

The sciatic nerve may be damaged as a result of fractures of the pelvis or femur; the commonest cause, however, is a misplaced injection in the buttock.

Common peroneal (lateral popliteal) nerve

The common peroneal nerve runs around the head of the fibula and is most likely to be damaged at that site, the usual mechanism being external compression. This can occur in any damage to the knee or to the upper tibia. The nerve can also be damaged in patients in the lithotomy position if the straps are incorrectly placed.

Most common peroneal palsies resolve over a period of several months.

Mononeuritis multiplex

As the name suggests, this is an occurrence of multiple neuropathies, either sequentially or seriatim. These are usually caused by inflammatory conditions affecting the nerve, although they are occasionally seen in diabetes.

PLEXUS DISORDERS

Brachial plexus

The brachial plexus (see Chapter 1, Figure 1.3) is formed by the 5th, 6th, 7th, and 8th cervical and the 1st thoracic spinal nerves, although this is subject to some variation. If there is a contribution from the 4th cervical nerve, this plexus is said to be 'prefixed'. In a 'postfixed' plexus, there is no contribution from the 4th cervical root, but a major contribution from the 2nd thoracic root.

The spinal roots form into the anterior and posterior trunks which subsequently divide into the three cords (lateral, medial (or inner) and posterior). The lateral cord is formed by the 5th, 6th and 7th cervical nerves.

The medial cord is formed from the 8th cervical and 1st thoracic nerve. The posterior cord is formed by the posterior trunks from the 5th, 6th, 7th and 8th cervical nerves. From these arise the major nerves innervating the arm (median, radial and ulnar).

The plexus lies in the neck, behind the clavicle, and this forms one convenient way of dividing disorders of the brachial plexus, into those which are supra- (above) the clavicle and those which are infra- (below) the clavicle. Infraclavicular brachial plexopathies are by far the commonest encountered.

In upper plexus lesions (C5/6 roots/upper trunk), the affected muscles are primarily those around the shoulder girdle. When severe, the upper arm hangs uselessly, and is rotated so that the palm of the hand is visible from the rear (waiter's tip position). With less severe lesions, there are variable degrees of weakness around the shoulder girdle muscles.

In infraclavicular plexus lesions, there is predominantly involvement of the median, radial and ulnar nerve at a proximal level rather than as an entrapment neuropathy (see above, p 155).

The brachial plexus is particularly subject to traction injury, primarily because of the distance between the fixation points (the vertebral column and the axillary sheath). In the normal individual, the plexus moves with arm movement.

The plexus is at risk of open injury from gun shot wounds, etc, and from closed injuries, including birth trauma, falls, shoulder dislocations, improper positioning on operating tables and sports and traffic accidents. Surgical procedures occurring in the supraclavicular fossa also often produce a plexopathy. Radiation therapy is a well recognised cause of a brachial plexopathy, as is a neoplastic involvement, particularly secondary neoplasms arising from the lung (pancoast syndrome).

Neuralgic amyotrophy

This idiopathic form of brachial plexopathy is characterised by severe pain in the shoulder region, and is of abrupt onset. As the pain decreases over the ensuing 24–72 hours, there is evidence of weakness of the muscles innervated by the brachial plexus, with appropriate sensory changes.

In many instances, the condition is post viral and there is a rare familial form. Neuralgic amyotrophy has been recorded following lumbar puncture, following vascular imaging studies and hospitalisation for other medical or surgical procedures.

Thoracic outlet syndrome

This term defines a group of disorders in which the brachial plexus and or the axillary artery is compressed in the axilla. This may be caused by an extra rib, such that, when the arm is elevated, the artery and nerve are compressed. There may be a fibrous remnant of a rib producing a similar entrapment. In some patients, it is hypertrophy of the muscles underlying the brachial plexus (particularly the scalene group of muscles) which causes the entrapment.

Thoracic outlet syndrome can be divided into vascular, neurogenic and vascular plus neurogenic. In the vascular type, patients will be aware that a finger will suddenly go white and then will turn, via blue, to red. This is often precipitated by exercise and particularly by having the hand above the level of the shoulder. In the neurogenic variety, similar manoeuvres lead to paraesthesiae, affecting predominantly the ring and little finger, although other fingers may be involved. Again, the symptoms are precipitated by activity, particularly carrying. The neurovascular variety is a combination of the above.

It has been suggested that some patients with whiplash syndrome (see Chapter 4) develop a thoracic outlet syndrome due to traction of the brachial plexus, which accounts for their paraesthesiae, particularly in those patients in whom there is no evidence of nerve root entrapment in the cervical spine.

Lumbosacral plexus

The lumbar plexus is formed from the L1, L2, L3 nerve roots, with some contribution from T12 and L4. It lies in the posterior aspect of the soleus muscle and gives rise to the femoral nerve (see Chapter 1, Figure 1.4). The sacral plexus derives from L4/5, S1, S2 and S3, and its main nerve is the sciatic nerve (again, see Chapter 1, Figure 1.4).

Patients suffering from disorders of the lumbosacral plexus experience abnormalities affecting the proximal leg muscles (quadriceps/hamstrings), which are frequently associated with pain. Particularly when the femoral nerve is involved, the patient finds relief when having the knee flexed. Involvement of the lumbosacral plexus should be suspected following any abdominal pelvic operation, child birth, radiotherapy, diabetes, buttock injection, fracture dislocation of the pelvis or hip joint dislocation.

It is not uncommon to find bleeding into the retroperitoneal space, causing compression of the lumbosacral plexus, in patients with a bleeding disorder, either disease related (haemophilia) or due to the administration of anticoagulants.

DISEASES OF THE NEUROMUSCULAR JUNCTION

For practical purposes, only two conditions need to be considered, myasthenia gravis and myasthenic syndrome.

Myasthenia gravis

Patients with myasthenia gravis have abnormal fatiguability, that is, they develop weakness with repetitive exercise. The disease occurs in predominantly two age groups, in patients in their late teens/early 20s and in their 50s. In the younger age group, females predominate. In the older age group, the sex incidence is equal.

The typical presentation in the younger age group is for the patient to complain of intermittent drooping of the eyelids which may, or may not, be associated with fatiguable double vision. The disease then progresses to involve the oropharynx, with the result that there is difficulty in speaking and difficulty in swallowing. It can then spread to involve the limbs, where repetitive movements quickly fatigue the limb to the point of being useless, and it can involve the muscles of respiration so that the patient has difficulty in breathing. In the older age group, the majority of patients present in a similar manner, but the obverse progression is not uncommon.

The difficulty of making the diagnosis of myasthenia gravis lies in the fact that when the patient is rested they are asymptomatic. The common situation pertains in that a patient attends their general practitioner's surgery with a complaint of double vision but, by the time they have waited to be seen, there is no abnormality to be found. This leads to the average delay time in making the diagnosis being nine months.

The disease is due to an autoimmune attack on the post synaptic membrane, and the antibodies which mediate this attack can be measured in the serum in some 90% of patients. Repetitive stimulation studies will show a decrement of the compound action potential.

The disease is eminently treatable, in both age groups, by removal of the thymus gland (thymectomy) producing the antibodies. Thymectomy requires a thoracic exploration and is thus a major operation; patients need to be prepared, in the sense that they should be in an optimum clinical condition before thymectomy. This is normally achieved by plasmapheresis.

There is considerable evidence to suggest that, the sooner a patient has their thymus gland removed, the quicker they will recover, and the more complete their recovery will be. In patients operated on within six months of the onset of symptoms, the majority are asymptomatic by two years and require no further treatment. However, in patients where thymectomy is delayed beyond two years, it may take up to five years for patients to be asymptomatic, and many patients are left with residual minor symptomatology.

Myasthenic syndrome

This condition is also known as the Lambert Eaton myasthenic syndrome, and it is the pre-synaptic counterpart of myasthenia gravis. In this situation, there is impaired release of acetyl choline from the nerve terminal, which leads to fatigability of the muscle. Conversely, however, many patients can improve their function with repetitive exercise. This, however, is best seen on electrical stimulation and is less clinically apparent.

Patients present with difficulty in walking, often associated with dry eyes, dry mouth and, in the male, impotence. About 50% of patients have an associated lung carcinoma. In the remaining 50%, the aetiology is often obscure.

Treatment modalities for the myasthenic syndrome are evolving. Drug therapy with 3–4 di-amino pyridine improves the situation for the majority of patients. There is some evidence that plasmapheresis and steroids are also of benefit.

CHAPTER 13

MUSCLE DISORDERS

INTRODUCTION

The approach to take with a patient suffering from a muscle disorder is first to identify the distribution of the weakness and then to investigate the patient to determine the cause of that weakness. The history is of major importance, particularly the tempo of the progression of the muscle weakness, and also whether or not a family history of similar disease is apparent.

75% of patients with muscle disorder will have the so called 'limb girdle' distribution of weakness, that is, they have weakness around the shoulder girdle and around the pelvis. The latter causes difficulty in getting off the floor and many patients have to 'walk up their legs' (Gower's manoeuvre) by forcing their hands against their thighs and pushing the body up using their legs as braces and their arms as levers.

Muscle weakness may be either symmetrical or asymmetrical. When symmetrical, the disorder is much more likely to be due to an intrinsic defect in the muscle itself whereas, when it is asymmetrical, it is more likely to be due to a disorder of the anterior horn cell (see Chapter 1, Figure 1.2) supplying the muscle.

The majority of limb girdle myopathies are inherited and are due to an abnormality of the muscle membrane. For the majority of the limb girdle dystrophies, gene defects have been identified, though the protein product has not been as fully elucidated as that involved in, for example, Duchenne dystrophy.

DIAGNOSIS OF MUSCLE DISEASE

In the inherited dystrophies, diagnosis is both by muscle biopsy and by molecular genetic techniques. The absence of the protein can be demonstrated on muscle biopsy and the deletion, or other abnormality, of the gene identified by molecular genetic techniques.

Duchenne muscular dystrophy is the commonest of all the inherited dystrophies. As an X-linked disorder, it is manifested by the male and carried by the female. Afflicted boys show delayed motor milestones and never learn to run. Their most ambulant phase is between the ages of five and 10, following which, they become confined to a wheelchair; the majority die between the ages of 18 and 22. No form of therapy has yet been found to influence the course of the disease. At present, attempts to replace the missing dystrophin are under trial.

NON-INHERITED MYOPATHIES

The commonest of these is polymyositis, which, when associated with a facial rash, is known a dermatomyositis. This condition is due to inflammatory changes within the muscle which lead to muscle pain and weakness in a limb girdle distribution. The symptoms usually evolve slowly over a period of three to six months.

Diagnosis is by muscle biopsy and treatment is with steroids. These have to be continued for protracted periods of up to three years and steroid complications are therefore common.

POLYMYALGIA RHEUMATICA

This is a condition occurring in patients over the age of 55. It has an association with temporal arteritis (see Chapter 7). Patients present with diffuse aching pain in the shoulder girdle and, to a lesser extent, in the pelvic girdle, associated with marked stiffness. The muscles may be tender to touch. However, there is no true muscle weakness, apparent weakness being due to pain. The symptoms wear off over a few hours in the morning and rarely recur later throughout the day.

Since the disease occurs in the ageing population it is often well established by the time the patients complain, since a degree of stiffening has come to be expected.

The patients can be found, as in temporal arteritis, to have an elevated erythrocyte sedimentation rate, and treatment is with steroids, continued for about 12–18 months.

MOTOR NEURONE DISEASE

This may present as a primary bulbar palsy, as progressive muscular atrophy or as amyotrophic lateral sclerosis. In primary bulbar palsy, the first symptoms are those of difficulty swallowing and speaking and, eventually, phonation is lost and patients are unable to swallow.

In progressive muscular atrophy, weakness usually starts in one or other extremity, most commonly the lower limbs, with the disease ascending through one lower limb, then involving the controlateral limb and then involving the upper limbs.

In amyotrophic lateral sclerosis, there are the same features as in progressive muscular atrophy. However, there are associated signs and symptoms of a myelopathy. All three disorders eventually merge and their clinical distinction becomes academic.

In addition to weakness, patients frequently complain of cramps, initially provoked by exercise and subsequently occurring at rest. They also complain of fasciculations, that is, small flickerings occurring in the muscles, initially provoked by exercise and eventually occurring at rest.

The disease runs in an inexorable downhill course and death occurs between two and five years after the onset. The brain itself is not affected and the patients are aware of their steady decline. Treatment is supportive, swallowing difficulty being overcome by percutaneous gastrostomy. The possibility of using drug therapy, either to delay the progression of the disease and/or to improve survival, is being investigated.

Despite numerous claims, no antecedent trauma has been shown to be a causative or provoking factor in motor neurone disease.

CHAPTER 14

DEMENTIA

INTRODUCTION

Dementia refers to a clinical syndrome rather than a pathological entity, and describes patients with evidence of widespread cortical dysfunction in whom arousal is normal and who remain alert. This distinguishes them from patients with stupor or coma (see Chapter 5).

For patients to be described as demented, the disorder must be sufficiently severe as to interfere with social or occupational function. This, of course, implies that there is no simple 'cut off' between the normal memory failure of ageing and the profound memory failure that occurs in dementia.

Whether or not true dementia remains part of a spectrum of normal senescence has yet to be determined.

Alzheimer's disease, vascular disease (with our without features similar to Alzheimer's disease) and frontal lobe dementia are the major sub types of dementia, accounting for approximately 50%, 25% and 10–20% respectively of all cases of dementia seen.

Alzheimer's disease

This is a disease of middle and later life. Early onset cases are often familial. Typically, the patient presents with memory impairment early in the course of the disease and this, initially, is loss of memory of day to day matters. The patient will frequently mislay objects and show marked frustration when they are unable to recall their location. Since, at least in the early stages, remote memory (memory of early life) is preserved, the patients often tend to 'dwell in the past'. Subsequently, however, remote memory also becomes affected.

After the initial onset, disorders of spatial awareness develop, and the patient may well get lost on familiar routes from point to point, initially outside the house and subsequently within the house. Seizures occur in some 10–20% of patients as a late feature.

Neurological examination is essentially normal, apart from the abnormalities of higher intellectual function. In the later stages of the disease, return of primitive reflexes (pout, palmomental) may occur. However, it is axiomatic that a patient who presents with so called 'dementia' and shows an abnormal neurological examination, should be investigated in detail to ensure that there is no underlying metabolic or structural disorder which may account for the apparent dementia.

Modern techniques of molecular biology are starting to identify abnormalities in transport proteins within the brain, which may well play an aetiological role in the dementias.

At present, there is no effective therapy, although drugs are under development which are claimed to slow down the progression of the disease.

Vascular dementia

Patients who have frequent and increasing numbers of 'mini strokes' may lose sufficient volume in their cortex to appear demented. In the early stages, it may be possible to ascribe the loss of function to a discrete lesion within the cortex but, with passage of time and continued loss of cortical function, the picture merges into that of an Alzheimer's type dementia.

It remains uncertain as to whether vascular dementia is a true entity or is an incidental finding in patients with an Alzheimer's type picture as described above.

Frontal lobe dementia

This is a rarer form of dementia, where the patients present in a manner different from Alzheimer's disease. Their presentation reflects the area of the cortex which is involved, which is predominantly the frontal lobe (see Chapter 3). As a consequence of loss of frontal lobe function, the patients present with changes in personality and poor social conduct with lack of insight. They lose the overall surveyance ability of the frontal lobe and are unable to clearly monitor their actions, setting themselves unrealistic goals and failing to monitor their output.

This has a younger age of onset than Alzheimer's disease, presenting between the mid 40s and mid 50s. About 50% of cases are familial.

CHAPTER 15

MOVEMENT DISORDERS

INTRODUCTION

Movement disorders are generally considered to arise from disturbances in the basal ganglia. In simplistic terms, the basal ganglia can be considered as a 'damping system' between the impulses generated in the cortex and the impulse which finally arrives at the spinal cord. Thus, the basal ganglia monitor impulses arriving from the cortex and provide a feedback, via the frontal lobe, to the motor cortex in the form of a modifying function. Abnormalities of basal ganglia function can therefore lead to poverty of movement (akinetic rigid syndromes) or excessive movements (dyskinesias).

Akinetic rigid syndromes

The prototype of this group of disorders is Parkinson's disease, which is characterised by slowing of both emotional and voluntary movement, with muscular rigidity and tremor. The disorder has been shown to be due to a lack dopamine within the basal ganglia.

Parkinson's disease is a common disorder, the incidence rising after the age of 50 to somewhere between 1–2% of the ageing population. Presentation is usually between the ages of 55 and 70, and the onset is rarely, if ever, dramatic. In the majority of patients, there is a slow insidious onset of tremor, stiffness and clumsiness, typically affecting one upper limb. The voice becomes softer and may become slurred (dysarthria), and there may be difficulty in walking. Although the disease can remain confined to one side of the body for many years, it classically spreads to involve both sides of the body over a period of several years.

The typical patient has a mask like expression with a soft monotonous voice, they walk with slow small steps (*march au petite pas*), with impairment of arm movement. The greatest difficulty is in initiating movement, for example, walking or getting out of a chair, and the patient often tends to 'freeze' when trying to go through an open door or when turning.

The majority of patients with Parkinson's disease have a tremor which is often described as 'pill rolling' because of its rhythmicity. It is important to recognise, however, that not all patients with a tremor have Parkinson's disease. The diagnosis of Parkinson's disease is entirely clinical. There are no specific aids to diagnosis, as in other diseases where the diagnosis is clinical (for example, epilepsy: see Chapter 6). This allows scope for considerable diagnostic variability.

In one study of 100 patients referred to a neurological clinic with a working diagnosis of Parkinson's disease, only 54 turned out to have that diagnosis. The diagnoses of the remaining 46 comprised miscellaneous movement disorders, the most common of which was benign essential tremor (see below, p 171).

As noted previously, Parkinson's disease is due to a lack of dopamine in the striatum (part of the basal ganglia) and treatment is therefore directed to replace the missing endogenous dopa with exogenous dopa. In the early stages of the disease, this causes few or no problems. However, the longer drug therapy is continued, the more drug induced side effects will develop. This implies that the management of patients with Parkinson's disease should only be undertaken by those with specific experience in the field which, unfortunately, is not always the case.

Multi system atrophy

There are a variety of other akinetic rigid syndromes which have a Parkinsonian component to them, but in which the Parkinsonian features are only part of the syndrome. These various disorders can now be subsumed into the title of multi system atrophy (MSA) to describe patients who have Parkinsonian features with, in addition, combinations of extra pyramidal, cerebellar and autonomic dysfunction.

The two commonest MSAs are Shy-Drager syndrome and Steele-Richardson-Olszewski syndrome (otherwise known as progressive supranuclear palsy). In Shy-Drager syndrome, there are problems with autonomic dysfunction leading to postural hypotension. In Steele-Richardson-Olszewski syndrome, there is impairment of eye movements, and pyramidal involvement.

These two disorders must be distinguished from idiopathic Parkinson's disease in that their response to therapy is markedly different, as is their long term prognosis. Both of these diseases lead to marked shortening of the life span in comparison to Parkinson's disease, where life span is not shortened.

Dyskinesias

These disorders are characterised by excessive movement and can be sub divided into the dystonias, chorea, tremor, myoclonus and tics.

Dystonia

Dystonias are characterised by sustained muscle contraction, causing twisting and repetitive movements or abnormal postures, without associated neurological features. This serves to differentiate the inherited idiopathic dystonias from the secondary dystonias which may be associated with neuro degenerative diseases of the brain, head injury, drugs and metabolic disorders.

The dystonia may be generalised (generalised dystonia, or dystonia musculoram deformans), segmental (for example, affecting the arm and neck), or focal (for example, torticollis, blepharospasm and dystonic writer's cramp).

Treatment is generally unrewarding, although it is recommended that all patients who develop dystonia under the age of 30 should have a three month trial of dopa therapy to exclude the rare possibility of a dopa responsive dystonia.

Treatment for the focal dystonias (particularly blepharospasm and torticollis) has been improved by the use of botulinum toxin injections, the injection of which produces temporary paralysis of the over active muscles.

Chorea

Chorea is defined as flowing, irregular, purposeless, unpredictable and brief jerking movements which appear to flit from one part of the body to another at random. Chorea is commonly seen in two forms: an inherited form of the disease, which is associated with dementia (Huntington's disease), and following rheumatic fever (Sydenham's chorea/St Vitus dance).

Huntington's disease starts insidiously in the mid 40s with chorea and, in the majority of cases, proceeds to dementia. The molecular characterisation of Huntington's disease is now almost complete and thus siblings at risk of the autosomal dominant disorder may be screened to determine whether or not they carry the gene with the disease. If they do, they will inevitably express the disease, and this raises considerable ethical dilemmas.

Sydenham's chorea tends to occur in childhood following an episode of rheumatic fever and is obviously becoming less frequent as rheumatic fever itself becomes less frequent. It is thought that chorea developing in pregnancy (chorea gravidarum) is recurrence of Sydenham's chorea.

Tremor

This is defined as rhythmical oscillatory movement of part of the body, caused by rhythmical muscular contraction. This is a feature of all individuals, who will demonstrate a tremor of the outstretched hands, either spontaneously or in association with anxiety, infection or drug therapy.

The differentiation between a normal tremor and a pathological tremor may, at times, be difficult. The commonest form of tremor is that of a benign essential tremor which is a common mis-diagnosis for Parkinson's disease (see above). In this situation, the tremor is present throughout the range of movement and patients have particular difficulty, for example, in carrying a cup; although usually unilateral, it may be bilateral and may also affect the jaw.

Sixty to seventy per cent of patients find that their tremor is abolished by alcohol. In the majority of patients, the tremor may be brought under control by the administration of propranolol. The effect of alcohol is illustrated by the following case history: a 50 year old priest presented with a 12 year history of bilateral hand tremor. Initially, he had found this embarrassing but, having worked in the same parish for many years, his parishioners had become accustomed to his tremor and had ceased to pass comment. However, with increasing responsibility he also took a peripatetic role covering a large number of parishes. At that stage, he found that his tremor became intrusive and attributed this to the anxiety induced by facing previously unknown parishioners. The problem was overcome by his consumption of a glass of sherry one hour before a service was due to start, which rendered him tremor free for three to four hours.

Myoclonus

Myclonus is defined as rapid, brief, shock like muscle jerks which are frequently repetitive and sometimes rhythmical. As with tremor, this occurs in almost all individuals and includes hiccup (due to myoclonus of the diaphragm) and the 'jerk' which occurs when falling asleep at night.

Focal myoclonus may occur as a result of epilepsy (epilepsia partialis continua) or of spinal root or plexus disorders. Spinal myoclonus may occur following trauma or be due to tumour, cervical spondylotic myelopathy or multiple sclerosis or, occasionally, following spinal anaesthesia. Palatal myoclonus is usually idiopathic but may be seen in conjunction with tumour or multiple sclerosis.

Generalised myoclonic disorders are usually associated with encephalopathies, particularly anoxic/ischaemic insult (see Chapter 7). They are also associated with drug therapy and metabolic disorders.

Tics

Tics are irregular stereotyped repetitive movements or vocalisations which may be imitated. They are more pronounced when the patient is relaxed, in contradistinction to other forms of dyskinesis, which are more apparent when the patient is under stress and are relieved to some extent when the patient is relaxed.

The most severe form of tic disorder is that of Gilles de la Tourette syndrome where there are complex motor and vocal tics, usually associated with behavioural abnormalities. This is a disorder of childhood, usually occurring before puberty, and consists of tics involving the upper part of the body, such as blinking, head nodding, shoulder shrugging and sniffing. The tics vary in location and severity with time. The vocalisations which accompany the tics are those of grunting, barking or yelping. About 50% of patients will show coprolalia (the over use of swear words in inappropriate situations). This is a life long disorder, in which severity often diminishes with age.

CHAPTER 16

DRUG INDUCED NEUROLOGICAL DISORDERS

INTRODUCTION

An almost infinite variety of drugs may affect the nervous system at every level, due either to the direct toxicity of the drug, or to an abnormal interaction between the drug and the disease process for which it is being used. In many cases there is no proven causal relationship between the drug and the disorder.

Drugs associated with encephalopathies (see Chapter 5, p 85) include acyclovir (used in the treatment of systemic viral infections), anti-epileptic drugs (see Chapter 6, p 102), dopa preparations (see Chapter 15, p 170), antibiotics (cephalosporins, penicillin, sulphonamides) and drugs used in psychiatric practice, particularly lithium.

Such encephalopathies may progress through stupor to coma, particularly with benzodiazepines, barbiturates and the tricyclic antidepressants.

Seizures (see Chapter 6, p 95) may be induced by both local and general anaesthetic drugs and by many antidepressants, particularly tricyclic antidepressants and the antipsychotics (phenothiazines). Antibiotics are frequently associated with seizure activity, as may be radiological contrast agents and vaccines.

Paradoxically, headache is commonly induced by drugs which are taken to relieve the condition (paracetamol, codeine, ergotamine). The mechanism through which this occurs is unknown, although simple analgesia overdose will frequently engender chronic daily headache in both migrainers and non migrainers (see Chapter 10, p 141). Other drugs which frequently induce headaches are antidepressants, oral contraceptives and transdermal nicotine (used as an aid to stopping smoking).

Many drugs have a potential to induce a peripheral neuropathy (see Chapter 12, p 152). The neuropathy is typically that of a generalised motor sensory polyneuropathy. Such neuropathies are associated with chemotherapeutic agents, some antibiotics and drugs used to control heart rhythm (particularly amiodarone). Drugs acting directly on the nervous system, particularly anti-epileptic drugs, may cause a peripheral neuropathy, as may lithium.

Drugs may frequently interfere with neuromuscular transmission and produce what appears to be a myasthenic syndrome (see Chapter 12, p 161). This may be due to presynaptic local anaesthetic like actions (for example, propranolol) or post synaptic receptive blockade (D-penicillamine). Combinations of the above are seen with aminoglycoside antibiotics.

Drug induced myopathies are not uncommon (see Chapter 13), typically producing a symmetrical limb girdle syndrome which may or may not be associated with muscle pain (myalgia). The prototype drugs in this situation are corticosteroids and, although an acute myopathy developing over a period of several weeks has been reported, particularly in intensive care situations, a chronic, slowly evolving myopathy is typical. Although withdrawing corticosteroids may result in improvement of the myopathy, this is by no means universally the case.

The increasing use of cholesterol lowering agents has highlighted the potential for causing not only myalgia but also a frank myopathy, which may be insidious or hyperacute (rhabdomyolysis). It has been suggested that elevation of the serum creatinine kinase (CK, an enzyme liberated from muscle) may occur without signs of myopathy in patients taking these drugs and, if the CK is raised, this is an indication to or reduce or stop the drug.

Neuroleptic malignant syndrome (NMS) is a rare but potentially fatal idiosyncratic reaction to neuroleptic medications. These patients develop severe muscle rigidity, fever, altered consciousness, autonomic dysfunction and a massively elevated creatinine kinase. It has been estimated to occur in between 0.2 and 2% of admissions to acute psychiatric wards.

Four features must be present for a diagnosis of NMS: muscular rigidity, a body temperature of greater than 39°C, altered consciousness (ranging from confusion to coma) and autonomic dysfunction (rapid pulse, rapid respiration, fluctuations in blood pressure, excessive sweating or incontinence). Treatment of the condition is with Dantrium.

The commonest drug induced movement disorder is that of tardive dyskinesia (TD). This is a disorder of the face and, in particular, of the lips and tongue, where rhythmic chewing or pouting movements are frequent. It is due to chronic treatment with neuroleptics (for example, chlorpromazine and haloperidol). It is more common in the older population, increasing in frequency until the 70s, when its incidence reaches a plateau. It has been estimated that, after a year of continuous therapy, a patient with schizophreniahas has a 4–5% risk of developing TD. The prevalence in patients exposed to neuroleptic drugs is approximately 20%. Treatment is limited, in that, withdrawal of the neuroleptic often leads to a recurrence of the original psychiatric disorder, necessitating re-exposure to the neuroleptic drug which caused the TD in the first case.

This chapter does not attempt to be a complete review of all drug induced disorders of the nervous system, but rather to focus on those topics which have been discussed in the preceding chapters. Similarly to syphilis, drug induced neurological disorders must be considered the great mimics!

BIBLIOGRAPHY

Annegers, JF, Grabow, JD, Groover, RV *et al*, 'Seizures after head trauma: a population study' (1980) 30 Neurology 638

Bruyn, PJ, Kalawans, HL and Vinken, PJ (eds), *Handbook of Clinical Neurology*, Vol 57: Head Injury, 1990, Amsterdam: Elsevier

Chadwick, D, 'Seizures, epilepsy and other episodic disorders in the brain' in Walton, J (ed), *Disease of the Nervous System*, 10th edn, 1975, Edinburgh: Oxford, pp 697-739

Jackson, JH, *Selected writings of John Hulings Jackson*, Taylor, J (ed), 1958, London: Hodder & Stoughton

Jennett, B, *Epilepsy After Non-Missile Head Injuries*, 2nd edn, 1975, London: Hyman

King's Fund Consensus Conference, 'Treatment of stroke' (1988) 297 BMJ 126

Pearce, JMS, 'Post traumatic syndrome and whiplash injuries' (1995) 8 Clinical Neurology 133

Sibley, WA, 'Physical trauma and multiple sclerosis' (1993) 43 Neurology 1871

INDEX

Page numbers in *italics* indicate an illustration appearing away from its page